Think Your
Way to Happiness

Other Books
by Laurie Hyatt, Ph.D.

Silent Decisions: Awareness out of Tragedy

Think Your
Way to Happiness

Strategies for an Enjoyable,
Meaningful Life

Laurie Hyatt, Ph.D.

ISBN: 978-1-63183-919-1 - Paperback
eISBN: 978-1-63183-920-7 - ePub
eISBN: 978-1-63183-921-4 – mobi

Printed in the United States of America   1 0 0 1 2 0

∞This paper meets the requirements of ANSI/NISO Z39.48-1992 (Permanence of Paper)

This book is dedicated to…

My daughters, Heather and Laurie Grace. Both of you are so talented and so strong. I know that you will continue to add lots of wonderful surprises to my life and to make the world a much happier and more interesting place.

My granddaughters, Chloe and Sophie. The stylish fashionista and the gourmet chef, both of you bring so much Light to my life.

My heartfelt wish is that you are all ecstatically happy most of the time.

CONTENTS

INTRODUCTION

If you are looking for **specific strategies for creating happiness** that you can begin to use immediately, then this is the book for you. The strategies explained here are based on two basic concepts, **perspective** and **choice**. Your happiness depends on your **perspective**, in other words, **how you look at things.** And, believe it or not, you make a **choice** to be happy. Yes, the good news is that **happiness is a choice**. You create your feelings, positive or negative, based on your beliefs about yourself and the world and how you think about people and situations.

The point is that you can change how you think, and when you do, you change how you feel and you change what you choose to do or not do. So, instead of thinking that your happiness depends on what's going on outside yourself, you can shift your perspective and realize that your **happiness begins inside your mind.**

LIVE YOUR LIFE
FROM THE INSIDE OUT.

Living your life from the inside out is the key to happiness. Rather than allowing external forces, such as people or circumstances to dictate how you feel, you can decide that you want to feel peaceful or joyous or contented. You can change from creating negative, self-defeating, or destructive emotions to positive, self-affirming, constructive emotions. Let me add a disclaimer here...we are human beings and we don't do well with this 100% of the time. I sure don't and I've been into this for many years. But, let's say if you can change your thinking 80% of the time. Wouldn't that be great?!

Hopefully, being able to **change your thinking** is reassuring to those of you who battle negative thoughts and feelings. I know that what I am saying may be very different from what you previously thought, but actually no one dictates how you feel except YOU.

I know you've heard people say, "That just ruined my day!" or "She made me furious!" Maybe you have said it yourself. When we say something like this, we let other people control our lives, like a puppet on a string. In reality, though, no one has the power to ruin your day or to make you furious...unless you give them the power to do so.

You and I are in the driver's seat of our lives. No one can pull our strings unless we let them.

I started writing down the specific strategies in this book years ago when I worked as a Licensed Professional Counselor with my own private practice. My clients were all adults with everyday issues like depressed feelings, hopelessness, relationship problems, or feeling misunderstood.

Some disliked their jobs or were extremely unhappy in a marriage or felt angry or overwhelmed much of the time. One young woman told me that she felt like the weight of the world was on her shoulders. Many had painful, unresolved issues from their pasts, and many more wanted to make major changes in their lives but had no idea how to start.

I could go on and on with examples, but the reason that I am telling you this is that I'll bet you can relate to some of them. Or maybe something else is leading to your unhappiness, but you are reading this book because you are tired of being unhappy and you are ready to learn how to be happy most of the time.

Over time, I realized that I was giving my clients some tools that they could use to change their lives. I knew that they were expending far too much energy on situations over which they had no control, energy they could be using to **create joyful, purposeful lives.**

So, I wrote a little book called *Tools for Living, Taking Control of Your Life (2001).* In it, I explained 12 tools that I had been teaching my clients. At the time, I was facilitating two women's personal growth groups, in Ellijay and Dawsonville, Georgia, so I asked for input from the women in the groups.

Today, I am updating and expanding that book, taking away information that I didn't think was necessary and adding strategies and ideas that developed as I created agendas for the group gatherings.

This book is for YOU. You can take these ideas and apply them to your life and the situations that you experience every day. In these pages, I will introduce you to many "tools" that you can use individually, share with friends, or you can bring a group together for weekly gatherings with these strategies as the basis of your discussions.

When reading this book, take the time to think about the ideas and how they apply to your life before moving on to the next chapter. It takes some time to process the strategies and put them to use.

In my personal life, a series of life experiences pushed me to realize that I needed support, encouragement, and guidance. I drew some women together to help all of us to grow personally, emotionally, mentally, and spiritually. I created the topics and readings, and facilitated the discussions. We all shared what was in our hearts, learned to think bigger thoughts by reading books by many wise authors, and learning from each other. We grew spiritually by seeing life as much bigger and more powerful than we might have realized individually.

So, my mantra for the groups was…

OPEN YOUR HEART. EXPAND YOUR MIND. LIFT YOUR SPIRIT.

I know that when you utilize the ideas in this book, that **you can take control of your life**, have more energy, feel more vital, get a bigger kick out of life, and often even seem much younger! Because most of us expend far too much energy on unimportant matters…far too much energy that we could be using to forge ahead to bigger and better ideas.

Life is a wonderful gift. It is sacred. Every interaction, every experience, every gorgeous sunset. Life is meant to be enjoyed. I enjoy life more than most people, I guess. "Where do you get your energy?" is a question I'm often asked. Or "How are you so strong?" I have even had people say they are "living vicariously through me."

Yes, I have a terrific life. But not because my life has been easy. I have experienced tragedy, loss, and disappointment, just like you have. I am happy because of the way I look at life. I want to share this with you, so you can be happy, too.

I will tell you that you will still experience down times, disappointments, and losses. But you will be resilient enough to ride through them. I also want you to know that shifting your way of thinking isn't easy. You have had your own way of thinking for years, and making a big change takes a willingness to be open and flexible, a willingness to consider other ways of looking at situations, and a willingness to change your perspective.

It is **how you view events**…not the events themselves…that shape your beliefs, your thoughts, and that create your emotions.

How you look at things…

Chapter 1

What Can You Control?

Let's start by looking at what causes you stress. Think about the stressors in your life. If you are a note taker like I am or you just like to write thoughts down, you can list the **stressors** on a piece of paper. I suggest that you start with three issues that cause you the most stress.

Your list of stressors probably includes **people**. They might be people who are currently in your life like your children or your life partner or your boss. Or you might be stressed because of your wish that someone special would come into your life as a friend or a lover. Your stress may be associated with what someone said or didn't say or what they did or didn't do.

Money may also be on your list of stressors. You might be experiencing unemployment that you didn't foresee. You might not have enough money to pay the bills or you wish you had money to realize a dream like a new home or a trip. Maybe your rent or mortgage payment went up or your children require more money for school, activities, or clothes. Or a divorce leaves you with one income to manage on. Some of you may want to have more independence, which includes your own apartment or having enough money to realize your life's dream to travel.

Another issue that causes many of us stress is **loss**. Someone in your family passed away or a good friend moved 2,000 miles from you. Maybe someone you care about is experiencing a major health issue, losing their former good health, or you are facing a big health issue. I know from personal experience as a breast cancer survivor that stress is not just the frightening diagnosis or undergoing horrendous treatment, but you also face the huge medical bills that keep coming in the mail. A divorce is certainly a loss, perhaps missing the person who you shared a space with for many years or just losing life as you knew it and having to start again.

There are many causes of stress that I didn't list, but you can put them on your list. Stress not only has the potential to cause you mental anguish, frustration, and anger, it can also be detrimental to your health. Research indicates that stress can contribute to heart attacks and strokes, increased blood pressure, gastrointestinal problems, headaches, and insomnia, to name a few.

Now, let's look at your list of stressors. Of the three stressors that you listed, **how many of them can you control?**

Let me give you a shortcut answer for one of

your stressors, the one pertaining to other people. The answer is that **you cannot control other people.** This chapter is titled, *"What can you control"?* Well, it bears repeating that you cannot control other people. **You can only control yourself.** I know that it is tempting to search for an exception like telling yourself that people are sometimes controlled by being put in jail or that a baby can be controlled by being picked up and put in bed. If you have had children, you know that you may be able to physically move a baby, but getting a baby to stop crying is a lot harder. Anyway, yes, people are sometimes controlled when they are physically forced, but that doesn't usually apply to us.

So, let's just say **you cannot control what other people say about you or anyone else, and you cannot control the decisions that other people make.** For the most part, you cannot control other people, not your children, not your boss, not your life partner or lover, not your friends and acquaintances.

Why is this so important? Because you spend so much time trying to control something that you cannot control. We use up vital energy and we create negative, self-defeating thoughts, which leads to unhappiness.

Of course, we care about people, whether they are a part of our family or friends or co-workers.

But the reality is that if we don't like what they are doing or not doing, what they are saying about us or others, we cannot change it. You can encourage, guide, educate, expose someone to new ideas or places or projects.

But **you cannot control what they choose to do.** Just like you, other people choose what they say and do. And, as I know all too well from my experience as a counselor and a college professor, you cannot teach someone who does not want to learn or guide someone to a positive path if they don't want to go there. The problem is that we sometimes beat ourselves up over someone else's behavior, and we had no control over it. We take the blame or we get furious or we create negative feelings.

I wouldn't have chosen to be a mental health counselor or a college professor if I didn't think that what I had to offer could change someone's life. Yes, we have the power to effect change or instill new ideas or information or attitudes, but only if the person is willing to consider what we have to say. A counseling client must be willing and eager to do the work required, just as a student must put in the time and attention to studies, so that learning can occur. And that's what you cannot control.

Now, let's make it personal to you. When I talk about *living your life from the inside out,* I mean to **focus most of your attention and energy on what you can control**. Again, you can only control yourself. You can control what you say and do. You cannot keep people from doing what you wish they wouldn't do and you cannot make them do something that you wish they would do.

Oh, yes, it can be so frustrating to watch someone mess up. It can be so infuriating when someone treats you with disrespect. You can ask for what you want, you can attempt to motivate or caution someone, but they are going to do what they choose to do.

Please don't expect yourself to be perfect at this. Good grief, I have had years of training and experience, and I still lapse once in a while and start dwelling on what someone else is doing like I have suddenly developed magical powers to make them change course. So, let's say that you are awake for 16 hours a day and you focus 12 of those hours on what you can control. You not only will accomplish a lot, but you have not wasted so much time and energy trying to change something that you cannot change.

Now, what about **money**? Can you control your financial situation? Yes and no. Yes, perhaps you can change jobs if you are underpaid. Or, you can get a skill that will give you opportunities to get a better paying job. You could even work a second job, at least for a short time until you get back on your feet or until you pay off those nagging bills. You can choose a career that you know offers a salary that would give you the lifestyle you want and work hard to get the education or apprenticeship skills required. I know that if you are in poor health, that is an exception, just like there are many other exceptions.

But, for the most part, you can set out to make a certain amount of money and find the means to do it. Or you can choose to down-scale or simplify your lifestyle or live in a more affordable apartment or move to a more affordable city. You can eat more beans and less meat to save on your grocery bill. You can turn the lights off when you leave a room to save money on the electric bill.

I imagine that you might be saying that I am over-simplifying here, but **money** is an issue that you usually have some control over.

Loss is very different. When someone dies, you have no control over that. You don't have control over someone else losing their good health, either. When your life partner of many years wants a divorce and leaves, you can't control that. I have been through **divorce** and the **death** of my son and the **disease**, breast cancer. I refer to them as the three D's…divorce, death, and disease. **They all involve loss** and most of the time, we have no control over them. We do, however, have control over how we respond to loss. And it's not easy.

Loss is a tough one. Sometimes horrendously stressful and sometimes completely out of our control.

So, how in the world can you be happy most of the time when you have experienced loss? Hopefully, the next chapters will enlighten you.

IT'S ALL IN HOW
YOU THINK ABOUT IT...

In this chapter, I made the point that what you can control is "objective." You can either control something or you cannot. **What is important to you, on the other hand, is completely subjective.** You decide what is important to you personally.

Each of us differs in what we consider to be important. And, the same person may change in what is considered important over time. What you thought was very important when you were ten years old is probably very different from what is important to you now.

Chapter 2

What's Important?

When I was in high school, driving to Pal's drive-in to see and be seen was far more important than the great hamburger they made and the little plastic monkeys propped on the cup. Now, at age 73, a delicious hamburger holds more importance than "being seen."

You might think that certain possessions are deemed important by most everyone. Surely, nearly everyone thinks it is important to have shelter, whether it is in the form of a house, apartment, or houseboat. Not so.

Believe it or not, my ninth great uncle was **Johnny Appleseed**. I'm not kidding. His real name was John Chapman, related to me through my mother's family.

Johnny Appleseed really planted apple trees, but he did not always have shelter. As he traveled from one area to another, he often slept under the stars. What was important to him was his spirituality, which for him included being part of the creative process by planting apple trees and teaching others how to maintain them. Creature comforts were not important to him. When he bought land, it was to plant trees. Then he would move on.

Years ago, when I was living in a 600-square-foot log cabin in the north Georgia mountains, I made **a list of what I considered important, absolutely essential possessions**. My list included pen, paper, candles, incense, a tent, blanket, coffee pot and coffee, toothbrush and toothpaste, very few clothing items. Some of you may be asking, "What about a phone?" This was 1994 and I didn't have a cell phone yet, only a land line. So, no, a phone didn't occur to me. Seems funny now, huh?!

About 10 years ago, Larry and I lived in a pop-up camper before we found this little house with a big garden spot. We learned that we didn't need a lot of stuff. Actually, it was nice to have a tiny space to organize and clean, which allowed more time for enjoying the beauty of the outdoors.

YOU AS AN INDIVIDUAL DECIDE WHAT IS IMPORTANT TO YOU.

What is important to you may not be important to me, or anyone else. It is your choice based on what you like to do, where you like to live, what adds meaning to your life. If you decide that an object is important, then your happiness could be at least partly contingent on having that object.

Living a pretty minimalist life gives me a **sense of freedom.** That ability to be able to pick up and go is far more important to me than any house or object. Plus, it is important to me to live fairly frugally. Huge bills would make me lose sleep. But I have lived in a big house in a subdivision when I was raising children. At the time, it was important that each child have a bedroom, that the neighborhood was safe, and that the schools were good.

So, you see how **what's important can change with circumstances and responsibilities**. In 2015, I facilitated a women's personal growth group in Gainesville, Georgia. One of the women had the great idea to exchange items that we were going to discard, including clothing, shoes, books, household items. The book that was no longer important to one woman might be important to another. That was a fun activity full of freebies.

Some of us were de-cluttering our homes and the "swap" helped to motivate us. In that group, as in the two women's groups that I facilitated in Ellijay and Dawsonville in previous years, it was important to us to connect with other women who were interested in personal growth.

What's important to you right now could be to put more of your time and energy into your spiritual growth. Or you may have an environmental interest in saving certain species of animals. Or cleaning the earth's waters. Or learning Spanish. Or, camping in all the national parks. Or having your own business. Well, I could go on and on. Let's turn it over to you now.

WHAT DO YOU THINK IS IMPORTANT TO YOUR HAPPINESS RIGHT NOW?

What feeds your soul? What would add joy to your life? What would make your life more fascinating? What would add meaning to your life?

While you are thinking, I'll throw in another example. Most of us think that it is important to have a vehicle. Personally, I have the purchase of an electric car on my list when money allows. Yet, Gloria Steinem, at least at the time that she wrote her autobiography, did not own a car. She expressed in her book how she connected with so many more people, which was important to her, by commuting all over the world by bus or train or whatever.

For some of you, it is important to have a steady 9 to 5 job with benefits. Some of you would be miserable in a job with structured hours, so you choose to run your own business and make your own work hours. Some of you might consider living together with a life partner to be necessary to your happiness and some of you are completely contented living alone without the issues that can cause tension when two people live under the same roof.

For me, of course, family is important. My friends

are important. And I can't imagine my life without my garden. Digging in the dirt is important to me not just for sustenance, but because I see myself as a vital part of the creative process of planting the seed, nurturing the growth of the seed into a plant that bears vegetables and fruit, and then being fortunate enough to eat natural and nutritious food. I am literally an important part of the cycle of existence. Gardening is an expression of my spirituality. But there was a period of time in my life when I could not be bothered with gardening. My life then was too intensely caught up in getting a job and thinking of ways to meet people, like starting a book discussion group.

So, we all change. Now then, what is important to you? Certain people, certain places, certain experiences, certain possessions? Really strip it down to what is REALLY important to you. Make a mental note or a tangible note.

OKAY, NOW LET'S PUT CONTROL AND IMPORTANCE TOGETHER.

Let's see how important the concepts of control and importance are to your happiness. This time, I want you to imagine a grid with four squares, or if you like to literally write like I do, draw the grid on a piece of paper. At the top of the squares write horizontally "Control" and to the right of that, write "No Control." To the left of the grid of squares, write vertically Important" and below that "Not Important."

So, your squares represent four possibilities: Control and Important, Control and Not Important, No Control and Important, and No Control and Not Important.

Think of your first stressor and number it "1." Let's say your first stressor is that your child has not chosen the career field that you wanted. Can you control it? Remember, the answer is "No" if it pertains to other people. Next, is it important to you? If you can't control the number one stressor and you have made it important to you, put the "1" in the first quadrant, which represents a stressor that you have "No control" over and you have decided is "Important."

WARNING! The quadrant, "No control" and "Important" is a danger zone! This is the land of fury and ulcers and heartaches. When you have no control over something, namely other people's behavior, and you consider it to be important, you are setting yourself up to be miserable.

The ideal grid includes more issues that you both have control over and you consider important. Examples are money issues, like a situation in which it is important to buy your own home and you can control getting the money to achieve your goal. The amount of stress is much lower in that scenario than in a situation in which you consider it important that a certain person behaves in a certain way, and, guess what, you have no control over it. That causes lots of stress.

So, the point is to examine what is stressing you and attempt to make the issues that you have no control over less important to you. Instead of focusing on the day to day happenings and events in other people's lives as all-important, **focus on what you can make happen**. It is tempting to spend time and energy complaining about how badly someone talked to you, for example, but unless you can take an action that will change that, it would be better to concentrate on making more money for that dream vacation.

One of the ingredients of depression is feeling helpless. Most people who suffer from depression feel as if they do not have the personal power to effect change. They are not happy with the way things are, but they think they are helpless to change it. So, focus most of your energy on what you can change.

The solution is to *look at life from the inside out*. Focus first on your own heart, your own mind, and your own spirit, rather than focusing on what is outside of you. Considering what's outside of yourself, like people and events, to be of paramount importance is an instant formula for producing hurt, sadness, and frustration.

Frankly, people are going to do what they want, whether you choose to allow that to anger you, hurt you, or make you absolutely furious. You end up simmering in a brew of negative, self-defeating feelings while the other person goes his merry way, oblivious to your pain.

There are some situations that go automatically in the "No control" and "Important" category. An example is the death of a loved one. You had no control over the fact that they died and, of course, it's important because you loved that person deeply. Unfortunately, those are the circumstances that we just have to learn to live with and they especially include loss. It's not easy, but we all have the power to heal.

So, to sum up these strategies for achieving a happier life, it is better if you let as much go as you humanly can and concentrate your energies, for the most part, on what you can control. There is a terrific example in one of Carlos Castaneda's books that makes this point. Carlos, the young anthropology graduate student and apprentice to Juan, the wise elder Yaqui Indian, asked Juan, "Are you angry with me?" Juan replied immediately that, of course, he was not angry. He explained that in order to feel angry, you must think that what the other person did was important to you. He further explained that over the years he had learned not to think that way anymore. He spent his energy on his purpose in life, which was to teach his spiritual beliefs. Specifically, his purpose was to teach his beliefs to an apprentice who would carry on his mission after he was gone.

Now, this way of thinking is not an easy feat. But it's a goal to work toward. Interpret what other people do as less important to you. ***Live your life from the inside out***. Don't depend on others to make you happy. Happiness comes from within. You decide whether or not you will be happy, no matter what deck of cards life hands you. You decide whether to make the best of it or to feel sorry for yourself.

And you decide how you view yourself, whether to love and cherish yourself in spite of your flaws or to see yourself as incapable of love and respect and happiness. In the next chapter, we will talk about how we talk to ourselves, about ourselves.

Chapter 3

What Do You Tell Yourself…about Yourself?

LOVING AND CARING FOR YOURSELF IS A FOUNDATION BLOCK OF A HAPPY LIFE.

The good news is that you can control how you view yourself. You can change your opinion of yourself. And you can choose to use only positive, helpful, self-affirming words when referring to yourself.

You will experience an immediate **shift in your attitude** toward yourself when you use words that are motivating and encouraging. Self-talk is powerful. Words are powerful. I'm going to be very specific now. Starting right now, right this instant, refrain from including the absolutes "good" and "bad" in your vocabulary. Never again say judgmental words like "stupid," "crazy," "loser," and "dumb" when describing yourself or anyone else. Judging yourself with derogatory words like these certainly isn't helpful in fostering a happy outlook.

There is a tendency to refer to ourselves as bad when we have done something that we consider to be bad. Or to chastise ourselves as stupid when we make a choice that did not get the desired result. No person is bad. **People are spiritual beings.** We are capable of creating light and sharing that light with others. As long as you talk to yourself in negative terms, you will create helpless and hopeless feelings about yourself. But the main truth here is that it is not true. It is not true that you are dumb or crazy. You may do something that you wish you hadn't done and there were negative consequences to your choice. But you are not personally crazy.

One of my clients years ago told me her story and then asked me, "You think I'm crazy, don't you?" Another version from other clients was "I know this sounds crazy, but…" It sometimes took several sessions of working together before they learned that I did not think they were crazy and what they told me did not sound crazy. They were just human beings living life and having experiences. I sincerely had no judgment about their behavior.

Sometimes it takes a while to get out of the habit of referring to yourself in negative terms. Just be aware of what you are saying to yourself. **Thinking in positive terms creates positive feelings about yourself. This is something that you can change right now.**

PHRASES THAT I
SUGGEST YOU NO LONGER USE.

They include "I should," "I ought to," "I need to," "I've got to," and "I have to." These phrases put a lot of pressure on you and, again, they are judgmental. Rather than saying to yourself, "I should help her figure out what to do," it would be better to say something like "I think I will help her figure out what to do." See the difference? Gone is the pressure to take a certain action. And the inference that if you don't help her, then you are somehow remiss is gone. Who said you should? Who decided that?

And in terms of the "have to" phrase, you actually don't have to do anything at all. Oh, my gosh, really?? Yes, really. You could choose to sit in your favorite chair for hours or days doing absolutely nothing. Oh, there might be consequences for that choice, like losing your job, but it really is your choice. This is a very freeing concept. We are so used to telling ourselves, "I have to do this" and "I have to do that," that it doesn't occur to us that what you are doing or not doing is actually a choice. Hopefully, when you wrap your mind around this one, you will experience a sense of personal power.

When you talk to yourself using less judgmental words, **you are treating yourself with respect.** You are giving yourself credit for making all the choices in your life. Now, on the flip side, there is some accountability here. You are making the choice, and you will reap the consequences. But now you are in the driver's seat of your life. Even though the responsibility may seem daunting, you are seeing yourself as a person who is capable of making constructive decisions.

LIST FIVE OR SIX WORDS THAT YOU WOULD USE TO DESCRIBE YOURSELF.

If you interviewed for a job, what descriptive words would you hope your interviewer would use to convince the big boss to hire you? What if the interviewer asked you to describe yourself in five or six words? What would you say?

Of course, you would **list your attributes.** You would tell the interviewer what your strengths are. As you incorporate positive words into what you say to yourself, **focus on your strengths.** Sometimes when I'm jogging and I start to get that awesome "runner's high" where I feel as if I could almost fly, I say to myself, "I am strong. I am powerful" over and over. The words energize me and I realize that the jogging gets easier and I feel lighter.

Okay, so let's say that you are just not feeling the positive vibe words right now. How do you get there? Here's how…act as if. Act as if you are smart. Act as if you are strong. Start with small steps. Have you ever done anything that made you proud of yourself? **Focus on the moments in your life when your actions got you what you wanted.** Then tell yourself, "If I could do that, then I can do this."

You are probably waiting for me to get to the "I can't" scenarios. Obviously, telling yourself that you can't learn a skill will not result in you learning the skill. Personally, I tend to balk on learning new technical skills with my computer or iPhone. But then, I tell myself how much more interesting and fun my life will be when I know how to connect the music on my phone to my new cute little speaker that changes colors. And, sure enough, it was really fun the other night when I was dancing on the porch and watching my speaker change colors. If the "want to" is strong enough, I will learn something new. You can, too.

I know you've heard a friend say, "I could never do that." They might specifically be saying, "I could never learn to speak Spanish," for example, or "I could never have my own business." When I had an office in Douglasville, Georgia, years ago, I remember a client telling me that one of her dreams was to travel to France. "Why don't you?" I asked. "Oh, I'll never have the money," she replied. Well, **that was a self-fulfilling prophecy.** If you don't believe that you will go to France, guess what, you're right. You won't travel to France or anywhere else because you don't believe that it is possible.

BELIEVING IN YOURSELF AND YOUR ABILITIES IS ANOTHER STEPPING STONE TO HAPPINESS.

Years ago, before I had my Ph.D., I attended a motivation program that had about six participants. I liked the small size of the group because we individually worked on what we wanted to accomplish. I was starting to think seriously about going to a university and earning the Ph.D. that I had thought about for years. I knew that I was capable of completing the requirements, but I hadn't distilled how the timing would work. Now my children were adults and the dream seemed to be getting closer to possible.

Anyway, the facilitator taught us a little trick that has helped me immensely. She suggested that we think of ourselves as having already accomplished our chosen goal and give it a time frame. So, I wrote something like, "It is May, 2007, and I have earned my Ph.D." This made the dream real. I could now say to myself, "You can do this!"

Telling yourself that you can accomplish your goals will probably have positive results. Telling yourself that you will have completed your mission by a certain date really motivates you and instills confidence. I have been working on the ideas and organization for this book for a long time, but when I gave myself a completion date, I really started to work more diligently. There is a literary festival in Blue Ridge, Georgia, a quaint town in the north Georgia mountains a few months from now. I was planning to attend to meet more writers and network. Once I decided to have this book written by then so that I could pitch it while I am there, I had my timeline. What started out being an idea in my mind will soon to be a real book. Why? Because I told myself that I would complete the writing phase of completion by a certain date. I told myself that I am capable of completing the writing in a specific time frame.

YOUR SENSE OF PERSONAL POWER HINGES ON YOUR BELIEFS ABOUT YOURSELF.

Your personal power is not contingent on anything external. You decide to be powerful. You tell yourself that you are powerful and capable. And then your determination pushes you to take action.

Change can be exciting. It can also be a bit frightening. With a new, positive perspective on yourself and your life, you can be energized by challenges. **You can shift your thinking and focus on what really matters to you**. The way you think and what you think about determines what you do.

Be compassionate toward yourself. Sometimes we don't treat ourselves very well. You can shift to no longer judging yourself negatively and instead talk to yourself with understanding and acceptance.

We all have setbacks. I was just talking to a wise man yesterday who pointed out to me that most of us wish we had a "do over" for certain times in our lives. He's so right. But then our conversation evolved to the fact that we just have the present moment. Well, here we are in the present moment, and we can decide to treat ourselves like we would treat a beloved friend.

If you moved to another state, you would probably make some new friends. How would you do that? You would attempt to find friends somewhat like you, with similar interests and dreams. When I moved to Gainesville, Georgia, for example, I searched for a writer's group. I found the Northeast Georgia Writers Group and now I have friends who are writers. Stimulating and inspiring guest speakers and enlivening discussions increase both my desire to write and my belief that what I am contributing is important. I told myself that it would be a good idea to bring other writers into my energy field and I'm glad I did.

What could you tell yourself that would add meaning to your life? How can you add a sense of purpose to your day to day routine? Time flies by and we are all tempted to get caught up in the daily mundane activities, like working, going to classes, shopping, doing laundry, preparing meals. It is helpful to your self-esteem to see yourself as very important…because you are very important. We are all unique and our individual gifts and talents are essential to the continuation of the big web of existence. What do you plan to contribute to the big picture?

When I sit in my garden and watch the bees happily pollinating one bloom after another, I realize that they are essential to the survival of the planet. Have you ever thought about your life like that? You were brought to this planet at this time for a reason. You have a purpose for being here. What is it? What it is that gives your life meaning doesn't have to be all serious, either. It can be fun. I really believe that part of the big plan is to feel fulfilled, to enjoy life, and to be happy.

Do you tell yourself that you deserve to be happy just because you are you? Look at nature. The butterflies in my garden happily flit around the delicate red trumpet-like blooms on the vine that climbs my garden fence. They know that their purpose is to pollinate the plants and they seem to be having fun as they work. The vegetable seeds know to burst through the ground and produce leaves and then tomatoes and green beans, as they utilize the sunshine and fresh air and the rain for energy. They thrive and produce and so it goes. To me, the cycle of life is so fascinating and I am lucky to be a part of it.

Have you ever had a magical day where every interaction was an interesting surprise, the necessary chores were not drudgery, and you met the most interesting people in the most ordinary places? I love it when that happens. It feels like I was destined to cross paths with that person or to find that particular book or to see that beautiful cloud formation. Days like that are so meaningful and underscore how we are all connected. All of our lives matter. We all have a purpose.

You make a difference just being you. There's been a lot of well-deserved attention to the late Fred Rogers lately. One of his greatest contributions, in my opinion, was his daily mantra, **"I like you just the way you are."** You are special. My hope for you is that just as Mr. Rogers told children that he cared about them and accepted them for who they are, that you will tell yourself that you are special, too.

Tell yourself every day how special you are and how important you are. **You contribute to the quality of other lives just by being you.** Be happy with yourself. Sometimes it can be tempting to be envious of someone else because they have a bigger house or more money or more stylish clothes. But those superficial aspects of life are not the good stuff. Happy people get up in the morning, grateful for another day on this beautiful planet, appreciating another opportunity to just enjoy being alive.

Live your life from the inside out…

Chapter 4

Who's Got the Power?

People who have personal power know that they have choices. Or, you could say it another way: Knowing that you have choices is empowering. ***Happiness is a choice.*** Remind yourself of this fact every day. You can choose to be happy. Your personal power is created from your ***perspective*** on what personal power looks like. I'm going to throw in some strategies here to help you increase your personal power.

PERSONAL POWER
VS. POWER OVER

Your goal is to increase your *personal power*, which will add to your happiness. When you are in control of yourself from the inside, that's personal power. When you allow someone to control you from the outside, then you are giving that person power over you. In general, humans gain a personal sense of power by either having power over others or by knowing that they are powerful themselves. Having power over someone else is not emotionally healthy…for the person who is being allowed to be

Laurie Hyatt, Ph.D.

in control or for the person who is allowing someone to control them.

When you know that you are powerful, then
you no longer allow others to have power over
you. By that, I mean that you do not allow someone
to control your feelings or your actions. The lesson
here is that you create your own feelings and you
alone determine what you do or do not do.

Let me give you some examples. It is tempting to
resign yourself to saying, "If it weren't for him, I
would do things differently. I wouldn't still be
making those mistakes." Or, "If my parents had
spent more time with me, then I would make better
choices." Or, "If the teacher didn't hate me, I would
make a better grade." When you think like this, you
are giving away your power. You are copping out
when you delude yourself into thinking that other
people still determine and control how you feel and
what you do today. **Let the past go.** Realize that in
the present moment, **you are in control of you.** You
determine what you decide to do, what choices you
make, and how much you study.

Other common examples are, "She made me so
mad!" or "When he called and told me that, it
ruined my day," or "You hurt my feelings when
you said that." Am I hitting a little close to home?
Don't worry, many of us say something similar.
We have this erroneous belief that other people
control how we feel. And think how powerless you

are when you say that. You are giving outside forces control over whether or not you are angry, over whether or not your day is ruined, and over whether or not you suffer with hurt feelings.

Here's how to use different, more constructive, positive words so that you create more positive feelings and you create an enjoyable day, in spite of others' remarks or behaviors. Don't say, "She made me so mad." Instead, begin by saying, "I allowed my boss to ruin my day" and then progress to "I chose to have my day ruined," and, finally, you will be saying, "No one can ruin my day." Don't allow anyone to dictate what kind of day you will have. Take the reins.

So, you're probably saying, "Yeah, right! I just decide not to have angry feelings or hurt feelings. In my dreams." I admit that this sounds like a stretch. But, yes, it is possible. And think how much more "in control" you will feel when you learn to use this strategy.

It goes back to what we talked about in the last chapter. Be aware of what you tell yourself and how you choose, yes, I said *choose*, to respond to others' remarks and behaviors. I know that these tools require skill, just like a mechanic knows what tools to use to repair a particular mechanical problem. You can master these skills and be in control of your life.

BE AWARE OF WAYS
THAT OTHERS CONTROL YOU

Let's explore specific ways that other people attempt to have control over you. There are several ways that other people can take control. The most obvious is by **intimidating you** by threatening, yelling, and calling you derogatory names. Or, actually physically hurting you. These people probably actually feel helpless themselves. They think that they have to show you their authority in order to scare you into complying. They threaten you in order to frighten you. They call you names, thinking that you will believe that you are the cause of their pain. They want power over you.

Change your thinking. People who try to intimidate you really feel helpless and inadequate. They wouldn't think that they have to hurt you or talk to you in a disrespectful manner if they thought that they had control over their own lives. Please don't feel sorry for them. Don't "put up with it," either. There are actions that you can take, like avoiding or getting away from that person. And, take it from a former counselor who worked in a battered women's shelter, the situation will only get worse. It will not get better without intervention.

Also, tell yourself that their out of control behavior actually has nothing to do with you. They may have learned to treat other people disrespectfully because it was modeled for them. But we are not going to take the time to analyze that, because I want to keep the focus on you. Feeling sorry for someone who intimidates you is not helpful to you…or to them.

Another way that people attempt to control you is by **asking sneaky questions** which have the agenda of finding you at fault, like "Where were you for so long?" or "Who were you really with last night?" They interrogate you like you are doing something without their knowledge or consent. This is a kind of silly example, but when I was living in the dorm at Pittsburg State University in Kansas, I got in trouble for being the instigator of a plan to change the overhead lights in the dorm halls to all red and green for Christmas. Well, the "powers that be" were not a bit happy with my radical lightbulb changing behavior and they literally called me into a room and questioned me like I had committed a felony. At least, that is my memory of it, which I may have exaggerated with time, kind of like a fish story. Anyway, they were determined that I would confess to my crime, and I did, not thinking, frankly, that it was a big deal.

A third way that people can control you is by being **aloof and mysterious.** In my experience, this is a typical technique used by men and women to get your attention. They purposely don't let you into their life, don't tell you where they are or what they are doing. They disappear for days without a word. Or "ghost" you by acting like they had a great time with you, only to never be heard from again. What often happens is that you start second-guessing yourself, like asking what you did to make them mad or to drive them away or to lose their interest. You spend time waiting by the phone, hoping he will call. "Where is he?" you ask yourself, and "Why doesn't she call me or text me?" Finally, you figure out that it is a game played by a person who is probably narcissistic.

The fourth way that some people control your feelings and actions is with **self-pity.** When people feel sorry for themselves, they draw others in to show them sympathy. The secondary gain for them is they get more attention. Now, you are worrying about them and doing things for them that you wouldn't do otherwise. Be very careful with this one. The self-pity game works on many of us who are kind and want to be helpful. You get hooked. Watch out! Sure, we want to help others, but self-pity is a destructive way of thinking for others and for you.

Feeling sorry for yourself just depletes you of energy and fosters feelings of helplessness. Feeling sorry for someone else gives them the message that they are sort of pitiful and need you in order to feel better about themselves. It is one thing to have sympathy for others who are ill or are in a financial tight or who have lost a loved one. It is totally different if that person is using, consciously or unconsciously, the self-pity to control you. In that case, your "help" is really not helpful. You may inadvertently give the person the message that they do not have the personal power or resources to make it without you. You are not doing them a service, and you sure aren't taking care of yourself if you play into their manipulation.

PEOPLE WITH LOTS OF PERSONAL POWER DON'T ALLOW OTHERS TO HAVE POWER OVER THEM

People with lots of personal power don't allow others to have power over them. And, they certainly don't need to have power over others in order to feel powerful, or even adequate. You know how you sometimes come in contact, personally or professionally, with someone who is wealthy, but they don't need to flaunt it? They don't attempt to have power over you. In fact, if you hadn't gone to their big home on 300 acres or their place of business with 200 employees, you wouldn't have known by their demeanor that they were rich. They are what I call, "down to earth."

There's a funny story about Sonny Vanderbilt, which is probably not literally true, but it makes a point. Sonny Vanderbilt, who did not feel the need to dress up every time he went out in public, walked into a furniture store with the intention of buying a dining room set. Because he didn't dress up, but instead chose a casual style kind of like the head of Facebook, the salespeople did not think he was financially able to buy their furniture. They figured he didn't have much money, so why expend a lot of energy trying to make a sale. Well, the old pro knew to introduce himself to everyone who came in the store, because you never knew who was a serious customer and who wasn't. He, of course, made a big sale. It's kind of refreshing when someone has so much personal power that they don't ignore someone else or treat them with disrespect.

People with personal power don't need to steal energy from others because they have plenty of their own. In fact, they have so much energy that they are eager to give some of it to others, to build them up, not to tear them down. Imagine that you can see "power." Picture your own personal power emanating from your body and interacting with the energy force fields of others. Sometimes you can actually feel it when someone is trying to crush your energy, and you will learn to avoid that person. It's all about power and control.

I want to remind you that we humans are not perfect and we are not machines. We get tired and "sucked in" once in a while. Just dust yourself off, give yourself a little smile in the mirror, and say, "Gotcha!" to yourself and realize that we all get caught sometimes.

You know what personal power is about?

CHOICES. You have a choice in almost everything. In most cases, you choose how you are going to respond to negative comments, what you will wear in the mornings, what city you will live in, what people you will associate and which ones you will choose to let go.

Do you remember the movie, *The Truman Show*? There is a great scene in the movie where the main character and his friend are sitting on a hill, having a beer. The main character, who is beginning to increase his personal power, asks his friend why he has always had the same job in the same city. The friend replies that it never really occurred to him to do anything different, to have a different job, or to move to another city. Our hero replies, "You know why people go places? Just to go there." His friend couldn't IMAGINE living anywhere else or doing anything else for work.

The main character had personal power and IMAGINATION. He could imagine himself leaving the confining town, seeing new sights, meeting new people. Yet, there was a conspiracy to keep him within the confines of the town walls. That is so often true of life. Others who do not have personal power will tell you that you can't do this or that. Or they will try to discourage you, or at the very least, not encourage you.

You are in control of not just your day to day emotions and actions. **You are in control of your**

destiny. Once you start taking control of your emotions and actions and, frankly, ouch! taking responsibility for them, then you can move on to taking control of what you will do with your life. Limitless people take risks, knowing that somehow their needs will be met. They go off on adventures, knowing that the positive energy that they generate will be reciprocated by the universal energy. Limitless people know that they have CHOICES. They tell themselves, "I can sit here and listen to this negative diatribe or I can get up and leave" or "I can be miserable in this boring job or I can learn some new skills and do interesting work instead." "I can suffer through each day of not having the physical energy to climb the stairs or I can tell myself that I will eat 6 fruits and vegetables every day and start to walk 30 minutes or more a day so that I feel better."

Effective therapists do not tell their clients what to do. What therapists really do is to teach their clients to explore alternatives and new ideas, new ways of thinking. I'll give you an example of how trapped people can be when they have little personal power. A woman came to see me in my private practice. She wanted to leave her husband because he had become more physically abusive to her, to the point that her life was in danger. She had called the police and been hospitalized as a result of one of his recent tirades. When we began to consider her choices, she remarked, "I don't know what to do. I don't have anywhere to go."

After another 20 minutes or so of brainstorming together, she came up with four possible places where she could go immediately, if she chose. I hope in a relationship like this where the power is way out of balance that both people will get help and be able to change their thoughts and behavior so that the crisis will end up being an impetus for change. But, sometimes, you just have to make a loving decision to take care of yourself.

A crisis can be an opportunity to learn and expand your thinking. When you have personal power, you can weather the storms of life, see light even in the midst of darkness, and know that your emotions and actions are CHOICES that you make.

Who's got the power? You've got the power!

Chapter 5

What Energizes You?

This chapter is about what increases your energy. By energy, I mean not only physical energy, but also mental energy and emotional energy. I think that whether you are in a low energy or a high energy frequency, you bring situations and opportunities into your life that match your energy.

Your goal is to get yourself into a high energy frequency. When you are operating at full tilt, you feel happier, your life is more meaningful, and you experience more joy.

I have devoured two of Marie Kondo's books on de-cluttering your environment, *The Life-changing magic of tidying up* (2014) and *Spark Joy* (2016). Thanks to her wise advice, I have minimized my clothing, books, and papers, and I also organized all of my photographs into albums. Thank you, Marie! Many of you are probably familiar with Marie's now famous question which determines whether you keep or discard a particular item, "Does it bring me joy?"

Think about it. The article of clothing or the book, for example, does not contain innate joy. The joy comes from your personal interpretation of the object and its importance to you. Other questions that you might ask yourself to figure out if the item brings you joy are, "Does this blouse reflect how I see myself?" or "Am I attractive in this blouse?" or "Does this blouse project the image that I want to portray at work?" When you are deciding whether or not to keep a book or discard it, you might ask, "Is this book important to me?" "Does it hold information that is useful to me now?" or "Does this book still entertain me every time I read it?"

WHAT INCREASES YOUR ENERGY? WHAT DEPLETES YOUR ENERGY?

In keeping with our theme of creating a joyful, meaningful life, the clothing and books that bring me joy, for instance, may not bring you joy at all. So, it goes back to you. You **choose** what creates joy for you and you **choose** what adds meaning to your life. The joy and meaning are not contained inside that blouse or book. They are in your mind.

Do you feel energized when you put on that dress and look at yourself in the mirror? Are the ideas in that book so fascinating to you that you want to keep it to refer to again and again?

You create the joy based on your individual interpretation of the benefits or lack of benefits of that object. So, being aware of Who You Are is essential to making decisions about who and what you bring into your energy field. Does that person or that dress bring you or keep you in a high energy state or does it drag you down, or even trap you? What I mean by that is that too much stuff with no useful purpose just takes up space, weighs you down, and keeps you trapped in a house because discarding all that junk just seems too overwhelming.

WHAT PERSON, PLACE, ACTIVITY, OR DREAM ENERGIZES YOU?

For me, sometimes a movie's characters energize me with their quirkiness and comedic sense of timing. Think "The Marvelous Mrs. Maisel" on Prime Video, for example. I have to concentrate and focus to keep up with the main character because she truly does have a marvelous sense of comedic timing. Some books energize me because the author's ideas are so interesting and thought-provoking that my energy increases as I ponder deep thoughts. Think *Sapiens* (2015) by Yuval Noah Harari. I have underlined and written notes throughout this book because his statements like, "If happiness is determined by expectations, then two pillars of our society…mass media and the advertising industry…may unwittingly be depleting the globe's reservoirs of contentment." Hmmm…That statement pushes me to think. On a physical energy note, comfortable, supportive running shoes with a high arch energize me when I try them on, walk around, and literally feel a spring in my step.

What individual energy fields energize me are probably different from the human energy fields that energize you. I have been attracted to several Scorpio men in my life, including my sweetheart, Larry. They all had a magnetic pull for me because their intense energy was almost intoxicating, and was definitely hard to resist. Now, for you, those same men might drain your energy. But I like intensity. I am attracted to extremes. I like some degree of risk. For example, Larry runs his own home remodeling business. He works for himself, which is risky. I am energized by watching him initiate phone calls and then share his expertise with prospective customers regarding potential jobs and the materials required. You, on the other hand, may prefer a 9 to 5 kind of guy with a steady paycheck and benefits. The uncertainty of not being sure where the next dollar will come from may make your face turn pale.

My energy increases when there is an element of risk, a challenge. I like working for myself, too, rather than following the procedures and rules that come with working for someone else. Punching a clock and adhering to "This is how we do it here" throws my energy into a nose dive.

Years ago, after becoming a Licensed Professional Counselor, I went out on a limb and set up my individual private practice based solely on "self-pay." I no longer accepted insurance payments for my work with clients. As I reflected on what was important to me, I realized that I despised labeling clients. In fact, I felt that labels were a deterrent to their happiness. If you get payments from an insurance company for therapy, you have to provide a label with words and numbers, like the popular "mild depressive disorder 300.40." Okay, I get it that the label is a shorthand time saver, avoiding writing out the phrases "low energy" or "lack of interest" or "a sense of meaninglessness." But I think that each individual's uniqueness is better reflected by a rich description of the factors that brought them to therapy.

People are not their labels. Saying that someone has "a depressive disorder" or hearing someone say, "I'm bipolar" or "I have ADHD" seems too impersonal to me, and misses the huge scope of who that person is with their inherent complexities. Everyone is complicated and that's what's fascinating to me. There's the stuff of high energy. And I resonate with the word, "Why?"

Maybe you don't care "Why?" when you are at the doctor's office with symptoms that you just want to cease. That makes perfect sense to me. But I want to dig deeper. I want to understand why my blood pressure is high rather than just taking a pill. So, understanding the root causes of a behavior is important to me. You may care less "Why?" and just want to know "What?" to take to balance your health. There's no "I'm right and you're wrong" to our differences. We are all different, and what energizes us is different.

YOUR HAPPINESS IS LARGELY DEPENDENT ON WHAT ENERGIZES YOU.

Think about it for a minute. When do you feel most excited about life? What gets you up in the morning, eager for another day and another challenge? Or, does each day just blend into the next with nothing really exploding in your mind?

You probably know what I'm going to say next. **Shake it up!** Make some changes. You could start with just changing your environment, going through each room and being really aware of your energy level. You could get rid of stuff that takes away from a sense of order in your mind. You could try some new activity, like an exercise class. Or you could attend a new meet up to expose yourself to new people and new ideas.

For most of you, it's probably best to start small and build on the small changes, noticing what really energizes you as you go. Have you thought about how important "place" can be in energizing you? You may be a high drive New York City kind of gal or you may prefer a more rural, "grow your own vegetables" type of lifestyle.

You may be more **extroverted**, so you are energized by a crowd of people or you may be more **introvert**ed and feel more energized in small groups or especially in one on one interactions.

You may like spontaneity, like going somewhere at the spur of the moment without tending to all the details like where you are going to stay. Or you may like things to be more predictable or manageable, planning a trip with meticulous attention to hotels and meals.

You may like **working with people** or you may be happiest when you are **working with your hands.** The classroom with its hours of listening and considering theories may be boring and tiring to you. You may be happiest getting a technical hands-on skill.

What kind of music energizes you? What colors bring you excitement or tranquility?

Let's reflect on who you are and what energizes you. The payoff is that you will be much happier because most of the time you will be doing what you enjoy. I've mentioned some specific energizers, so let's take some time to make them specific to you.

Here are some questions for you. Let me add a disclaimer because I know you might answer with "It depends on what mood I'm in" or "It depends on how tired I am," for example. Just answer by prefacing with "Most of the time…"

1. Would you rather be outside grilling a steak or chicken or would you be happier in a nice restaurant?

2. Would you rather live in an apartment or townhouse with little or no outside upkeep or would you prefer to live in a house with at least a small yard?

3. Do you like shopping so much that you can spend hours enjoying just looking around or do you like to plan what you need and have a "get in and get out" approach?

4. Do the benefits of having pets as companions outweigh the responsibility of taking care of them?

5. Do you like overhead lighting or do you enjoy candlelight more?

6. Would you rather go camping or go somewhere and stay in a nice hotel?

7. Are you a meat eater or a vegetarian? Do you usually eat healthy foods?

8. Do you go to church and have a firm religious belief or would you describe yourself as spiritual without the desire for religious dogma?

9. In what ways are you creative? Artist? Writer? Cooking? Gardening? Interior design? Landscape design? Scrapbooking? Fashion stylist? Hair stylist? Marketing? Mechanics? Sculpting? Sewing? Coordinating events? Woodworking?

10. Is physical fitness important to you? What do you do to stay fit?

11. Do you like to read? Watch movies? Listen to music? Dance? Fix cars?

12. Are you handy, for example, can you fix plumbing problems or electrical issues?
13. Do you like outdoor sports like fishing, hunting, hiking? How about sports?
14. Is a lot of your time spent with family, raising children or caring for an elderly parent, for example, or are you single and living by yourself?
15. Does your dream life include travel? Or would you rather spend money building a new house? Or owning your own business?
16. If you had a million dollars, whether you earned it, inherited it, or won the lottery, how would you spend it?
17. If you could spend a day anywhere in the world, all expenses paid, where would you go?
18. Is there a skill that you wish you had?
19. In one word, how would you describe yourself?
20. What do you do for fun?

Reflecting on these topics will hopefully increase your awareness of Who You Are and what makes you happy, what you enjoy, and what makes your life meaningful. This is a fun activity to share and discuss with a friend or family member or you could create a small discussion group. The key is to take the time to know YOU.

Chapter 6

Words That You Can Live Happier Without

Transcending destructive emotions and ways of thinking will carry you far as you create more happiness in your life. The four words that I suggest you delete from your thoughts and your language are **hate, envy, jealousy, and resentment.** To change to positive thoughts, be aware of these energy stealers.

ELIMINATE "HATE" FROM YOUR VOCABULARY AND YOUR THOUGHTS

"I hate you!" "I hate him." "I hate how he treats me." "I hate it when someone acts that way." Easy to fall into using this word, "hate." Hating takes up a lot of energy. It's like you are renting room in your mind to the object of your vile feelings. You are wasting energy focusing your attention on negative forces. You are wasting time obsessing over someone's behavior that, here we go again, you cannot control.

Substitute the phrases "I don't like it when…" or "It would have been better if…" Can you see the difference in how tense you get, how you feel?

You're still expressing your animosity, but you are not selling yourself. When you spend your energy on hating, you create negative feelings that linger. You get yourself upset, and that feeling hangs around. While I'm not so naïve as to think that we can just completely let go immediately, I do know that letting go of hateful feelings will free you up to think thoughts that are constructive.

As I have helped women and men let go of destructive feelings and focus on what they can control, they have often shared the differences that just this change made in their lives. I often talk about **dreams,** because they **are our raw, unfiltered, uncensored thoughts and feelings** and you can learn a lot about yourself and what you're really mulling over by analyzing your dreams. Clients' dreams were often of an attic. They are throwing things away and sweeping out the attic. The sweeping was vivid, sweeping, sweeping, sweeping away what was being discarded, no longer wanted. **Cleaning out the attic in the unconscious mind is analogous to clearing our conscious mind.** It feels good to get rid of what is taking up room and serving no purpose. Believe me, you will feel much better when hate is cleared from your thoughts.

When your world is chaotic, it can be hard to imagine letting go of the forces that brought the chaos, that caused the disruption, that caused you so much pain. It might even seem like you're being too nice or too passive. What you are doing, though, is being kind to yourself. Keep the focus on you and how you feel and how you want to feel. You want to feel free, free of the chaos, free of the pain, free of what is trampling you down. I know it seems funny that by just changing the words that you say, peace of mind can be the result. When you hate, you are not changing the other person, you are not even getting back at them or messing up their life. You are just hurting yourself. You are wasting precious time and energy while the object of your hate is not affected.

YOUR HAPPINESS HINGES ON WHAT YOU THINK AND FEEL AND THE ACTIONS THAT YOU TAKE.

Envy and jealousy sort of go together. **Enjoying your life includes being grateful every day for what you have**. When you envy what someone else has or you are envious of their seemingly better lifestyle, you are again focusing on what is outside of yourself. You are irrationally thinking that "if only…" I had grown up in that family or "if only…" I had that much money, then I would be happy. So not true. I'll give you an obvious example. Think of an entertainer who is well known, who has millions of dollars, who lives in what you and I would consider a mansion, who has a gorgeous boyfriend or girlfriend, who tours the world performing or starring in movies. Now, give me examples of entertainers that you envy who are, in fact, miserable. I'm not going to name names here, but I know you can. What about "the star" who had a nervous breakdown or someone famous who is suffering from addiction? What about all of the messy divorces? You get the idea. It's easy to look at the superficial things, the homes and money, and be envious.

Being envious of what someone else has wastes energy that you could spend making your own dreams come true. Of course, the object of your envy may not be as "off the charts" as a Hollywood star. You might be envious of other people at work or at school who seem to have it all. Somehow, their lives seem to be easier than yours. They haven't had to work as hard or suffer as many disappointments or even tragedies as you. Maybe that's true.

Instead of having envy for them, maybe you can learn from them. You know, **we are all students and teachers in this life.** In any interaction, you could be the teacher or you could be the student. Maybe someone at work really is spending less effort and getting more productive results. Maybe someone at school really has figured out how to get better grades by studying more effectively. You might also learn that things are not always as they appear. The pretty young woman who seems to have everything may be unhappy behind closed doors. In any case, instead of envying someone for what…or who…they have or how they live, *it would be better* **to either learn from them, use them as role models or spend less time watching what they are doing**

Jealousy is another destructive, negative, energy-draining emotion. Most of us have wanted something or someone that we could not have. Most of us have wished that we could live with fewer temptations. It's easy to tell ourselves, "It's not fair." You can tell yourself that your life is harder, that what you are up against is more difficult, that no one understands what you are going through. You observe a co-worker who just seems to glide into a promotion or the acquaintance who just always seems to effortlessly be charming at parties. Or there is your friend who has been "happily" married for 20 years.

I will tell you with certainty that no one who lives long enough has a perfect life with no hassles, with no difficulties, with no heartbreaks, with no struggles, with no temptations, with no confusion, with no disappointments. It may seem that way, but your jealous feelings are only based on an illusion. I'll bet you have something in your life that others wished they had, like incredible children or artistic talent or work that you enjoy.

My daddy told me years ago that when you are tempted to feel sorry for yourself and think that others have it better than you, just look around and you will quickly see someone who doesn't. Daddy's favorite example was a young man who was in a wheelchair, with no use of his legs. In spite of how hard it was, that man went to law school and created his own law practice. His life story and many others can inspire us to focus more attention on what we can accomplish and less attention on what others are doing. We can learn from their perseverance and their determination. Instead of being jealous of someone else, we can take control of our lives and go after our dreams, grateful for the talents and the life that we have.

RESENTMENT IS ANOTHER DESTRUCTIVE WAY OF THINKING

I hope that you erase resentful thoughts from your database. When I was going through a divorce, I attended a one-night class on "Recovering from divorce" that was presented by a divorce attorney. Like many of you, I have been through divorce and I know from personal experience how difficult it is to navigate. I have been divorced more than once and I have experienced divorce from both angles. I have been the one who was deserted and I have been the one who left. Divorce is difficult no matter which position you have.

What the lawyer used as his theme for the class was RESENTMENT. He wrote the letters on a board in a vertical fashion and used each letter to make a point. I don't remember all of his specific points. The main idea was that **resentment is destructive.** Avoid being resentful. And the big news was that you can stop feeling resentment if you just think about your divorce differently, have a different perspective regarding the person who you were formerly married to, and create more positive feelings about your current situation.

As any of you know who have been through divorce or have had any problems in a relationship whether you divorced or broke up or not, blame is a key factor in how we create resentment. We blame the other person for the divorce or for the problems in the relationship. If it weren't for their selfish behavior or their infidelity or their lack of respect, everything would be fine. Of course, it could very well be that one person is more responsible or at fault than the other. An obvious example is infidelity. But even with the most difficult issues, and the really strong urge to blame everything on him or her, to say nothing of the mess it has made of your life, to hang onto resentment is just pulling you down.

No matter who caused the problems, continuing to blame and feel resentment only hurts you. **Resentment comes with a lot of baggage.** We spend a lot of time asking ourselves, "How could she be so insensitive?" "How could he treat me like that?" "How could he just keep on acting like nothing was wrong when he had to see how serious it was?"

Everyone I know who has been through a divorce and everyone who has complained about problems in their relationship has blamed the other person, at least for a while. It takes time, or an instructive class like the one that I attended, to shift your thinking away from blame and resentment and toward more positive feelings.

The main point is that resentment uses up your time and energy and it has no effect on the other person. Nothing changes. All you have done is make yourself miserable.

I want to add here that it is helpful and necessary to spend some time figuring out what went wrong, what dynamics attributed to the eventual break up. Even in a relationship that stays intact, it is essential to take time to analyze what problems contributed to the arguing or fighting. Hopefully, with personal reflection and then discussion and, perhaps, the help of a therapist or pastor, the issues can be resolved. However, as I know all too well, sometimes the most productive course of action is to go your separate ways.

Choosing sides is what usually happens in relationship difficulties. The result, of course, is resentment toward the other person. We all do it. But, after the dust is settled, the divorce is finalized, and the two parties have gone their separate ways, it is better to let go of the old resentments. Move on to establishing a new kind of relationship, especially when children are involved. A new business-like relationship helps the children because it minimizes volatile emotions. A new relationship based on working together to raise emotionally healthy children helps you in the "letting go" process, too. Whether children are involved or not, let go of resentment.

So, the nuts and bolts of this are to stop allowing hate, envy, jealousy, and resentment to take up space in your head. Sweep out the old destructive, time-consuming thoughts and feelings, and focus more attention on constructive, affirming ways of thinking.

What would that be? Let me interject a simplistic example here. If you had a toddler who was taking the books off your shelves and scattering them on the floor and you wanted her to stop, how would you do that? You are fooling yourself if you think you can just say, "Don't do that!" and the child will immediately obey. Ha! What really happens is that as soon as you turn your back, Susie is dragging those books out again. You can say, "Stop it!" all you want, and you know that Susie's fascination with the books is going to continue.

The most practical and expedient remedy is to place the books out of reach. In other words, erase the possibility of Susie reaching the books. Okay, child-proofing works. But, if you don't want to move your books, you can also distract Susie with a more fun, more productive activity. You could take her into another room, and place a really colorful and busy puzzle in front of her. Help her get started joining the pieces around the edges until she is now focusing her attention on the puzzle that you want her to complete. Presto! Now she has forgotten the books.

The same strategy, **shifting our thoughts to a new subject**, can actually help us adults to focus on going forward. After you have concluded that you no longer want to harbor hate, envy, jealousy, and resentment, then what do you think about instead? What thoughts and ideas would propel you forward toward joy and happiness? What can you do to get yourself unstuck?

How about re-creating your new life into one in which you are confident and focused on making a happier future for yourself?

Chapter 7

A More Confident You

How do you rise above life's adversities? *It's all in how you look at it.* Let me share a fun source of inspiration that we discussed in the Ellijay women's personal growth group.

Fun fact:

> *The bobolink flies 7000 miles from Canada to Argentina to migrate. He uses the navigational clues of the stars and the sun and the earth's magnetic fields to guide him.*

So, if a bird is informed by the stars, the sun, and the earth's magnetic fields, what guides your decisions and actions?

Getting to the point where you know what you want to do and figure out what you can do to make it happen takes self-confidence. What do you believe about yourself? Take some time to get clear about it, very clear. Like the bobolink is clear about where he's going and how he's going to get there. Having self-confidence makes all the difference in what you think about and what you choose to do.

And remember that your perception of events

determines what you think is the truth, what you think is real. For example, if there is really a snake in your yard, but you perceive it to just be a rolled-up piece of rope, then you won't respond with fear and perhaps jump away. But, on the other hand, if you hurriedly glance at a piece of rolled-up rope but it looks like a snake to you, then you might jump away in fear.

In the same way, **how you perceive yourself and your abilities determines your reality.** You make decisions for yourself based on your idea of who you are and what you have to offer.

When you *believe* that you can complete a project, then you direct your thoughts to how to make it happen. You start preparing yourself to take the necessary steps to get it done.

When I was in elementary school, my teacher gave me an assignment to memorize a poem which I just remember as, "Little Georgie Washington." The poem was based on a story, which may or may not be true, that when George Washington was about six years old, he was given an ax. He was so excited about cutting things down with the ax, that he cut down his father's favorite cherry tree.

My point in telling you this is that I practiced and practiced reciting the words to that poem. Actually, I also remember that Mother and Daddy and I were spending the evening in the backyard, where Mother was grilling hamburgers. I can't resist sharing another personal story with you. Mother, with a little help from 8-year-old me, actually designed and built the brick patio. Mother was artistically talented and she drew out the plans for the rectangular patio and the sidewalk that joined it to the back door of the house. A lot of red bricks and sand were required and I can still feel myself sweeping the sand into the spaces between the bricks.

Well, I started out telling you about all the preparation that I did so that I could flawlessly recite the poem to the class the next day. But now I realize that my Mother also prepared for hours to build that patio, taking measurements and figuring out what materials she needed, gathering tools, and then placing the bricks in a pattern, starting with the sidewalk.

And after she finished the patio, she created flower beds bordered with landscape timbers, filled it with dirt, and planted zinnia seeds. The result was a beautiful red brick patio surrounded by a thick blanket of red, yellow, and pink zinnias.

That project took a lot of self-confidence. That was about 1955 when a woman wasn't generally thought of as having the ability to design and build a patio. As I reflect back on this, I realize that before Mother could complete this patio, sidewalk, and flower box project she had to *believe* that she could. She obviously had the "want to" because of her desire to create a space in the backyard where our family could gather and have fun. **That was her mission**. Along with a belief in herself, she had to prepare to begin the work.

There are many quotes about the importance of preparation in achieving success in whatever you choose to do. "Measure twice, cut once" is one. There is also the story that is often attributed to Abraham Lincoln.

> *The story goes that Lincoln said that if he was given 8 hours to cut down a tree, he would spend the first 6 hours sharpening his ax.*

The moral to the story is, of course, that when you spend lots of time in preparation, you will feel more self-confident, and the results are more likely to be successful.

TEACHING A LESSON IN BUILDING SELF-CONFIDENCE

One of my favorite quotes is from one of Carlos Castaneda's books, *A Yaqui Way of Knowledge (1968)*. One day, Carlos, who was the elder Juan's apprentice, asked this question,

> *"Can a man really fly, don Juan?" Juan replied, "Why not?"*

Seeing ourselves as almost limitless, as capable of accomplishing almost anything with the belief that we can achieve success, is a sure sign of self-confidence.

Yes, believing that you can accomplish what you dream of doing certainly takes courage, willful courage and psychological courage. When you have a strong will, almost nothing can stop you from achieving your goals. And, psychologically, knowing that the sky's not even the limit certainly fires you up.

WISDOM IS A BY-PRODUCT OF STUDY, THOUGHT, AND REFLECTION

To increase your self-confidence, increase your wisdom and your personal power. Both wisdom and self-confidence result from attaining knowledge. Self-confidence certainly springs from attaining wisdom, being certain of your truth.

To be wise is

1. To be clear about your worth and gifts, so that no one can deceive you and convince you that you are anything less than intelligent, conscientious, sensitive, and a gift to this world from God.
2. To feel compassion for those who attempt to hurt you and put you down, while, at the same time, holding firm to self-respect and self-love.

3. To know that the truth about yourself is a decision that you make, and is not a reaction to others' opinions.

4. To share yourself with others by expressing feelings and thoughts, while realizing that it is best to be discerning about who will be receptive and non-judgmental and who will not.

This could be a pivotal time for you, a crossroads in your life. The decisions that you make today could affect your life for years to come. Your choices are limitless if you perceive that you have endless opportunities. Your self-confidence stems from knowing that you are wise, knowing that you are prepared.

Having the confidence to make sometimes drastic changes in your life requires a radical shift in your thinking. A huge shift like that happens when you change the way you usually think about things and start to think in a completely different way.

And you can shift your thinking right away, if you choose to. You can choose to believe that you are worthy, you are capable, you are important.

And with that self-confidence, you can do things that will help you realize and validate just how powerful you are. You have abilities that you have not even tapped. There are possibilities for your life that you have yet to imagine.

You're probably thinking, "Okay, this sounds great, but how in the world do I create all this self-confidence, all this personal power? How do I generate more self-confidence when my natural tendency is to focus more on my mistakes, my lapses in judgment, the times that I stayed in a situation long after it was helpful to me?" I do want to say here that, sure, it can be constructive to reflect on those times when our actions were detrimental to our happiness. But once you have gone over what happened and your part in it, then it is time to move on.

Moving forward is a lot easier when you have taken the time not only to assess how you could have done things differently, but to then assess what you need to do in order to move forward toward a more enjoyable life.

LET'S START BY TAKING AN INVENTORY OF YOUR STRENGTHS.

Many of you have important strengths that you don't even think of as strengths. You may not see what you do well as such a big deal, but others often see what you don't see. "Wow, look how talented you are!" is what other people are saying to you. But if you can do something really well that most other people can't do, you can capitalize on that strength to add enjoyment to your life.

When I was working on my Ph.D., one of my

classes at UGA was called simply "Creativity." My professor, Dr. Bonnie Crammond, made the point that what some of us see as ordinary daily activities are really very creative and require a lot of talent. One of her examples of being creative was the ability to cook an original soup recipe or a casserole that you created by adding your own combination of ingredients.

Maybe you cooked a delicious meal using your own ideas about what herbs to add and what combination of vegetables to use to make it delicious. My 17-year-old granddaughter, Sophie, is a very creative cook. She frequently experiments with different herbs and fruits and vegetables to add to a turkey. She also has her own way to make mashed potatoes and she adds rosemary and thyme to her special fried chicken. She is imaginative in the kitchen and that requires a lot of creativity and talent.

Or, maybe like my 22-year-old granddaughter, Chloe, you have a great sense of fashion style. I certainly don't have a sense of fashion, so it's particularly interesting to me to watch someone who does. I notice that Chloe spends hours studying magazines and media sites to see what's new, what's trending. Then she creates her own ensemble of tops, pants or skirts, and accessories and the resulting look id fabulous. She puts pieces together in her own unique way.

My granddaughters may or may not incorporate

their individual strengths into their career plans, but even on a day to day basis, their strengths add to their enjoyment of life.

Now, let's get specific about your strengths. Like my granddaughters, you probably have many strengths. I just mentioned one particular strength for Chloe and one for Sophie, but they have other talents, as well. You probably have many strengths, too. Take some time now to think about what strengths you have. To help you out, you might think about how your friends or family members would describe you.

Here are some questions that will activate shifts in your thinking.

1. Have family members or friends commented on a talent that you have?
2. Have family members or friends praised you for a particular accomplishment?
3. What would you do if you were confident that you could achieve it?
4. What would you do if you knew that you could surmount any obstacles in your way?
5. What dream would seem more realistic if you thought you were capable of making it come true?

Take a few minutes to consider the possibilities. This is about YOU. Your choices. Your passions. Your dreams.

Laurie Hyatt, Ph.D.

Let me add another quote from Carlos Castaneda's mentor to sum up this chapter. This one is from the seventh book, *The Fire from Within* (1984, p. 118) in the eight-book series. Juan said…

> *"They simply don't know about their possibilities."*

Chapter 8

Where Have I Been and Where Am I Going?

This chapter heading, "Where have I been and where am I going?" was actually an agenda theme for the Gainesville, Georgia, women's group a few years ago. I decided to ask the women to bring a photo of at least one of their ancestors to the next meeting. I thought that seeing the importance of our lives in the context of our family histories might be interesting and inspiring.

Each one of the women, in turn, showed a photo, and described that family member and their significance in their life. We all were surprised at how meaningful it was to take some time to think about our roots. **This was a tribute to those who have gone before us, and it helped us see our individual lives in a bigger context.**

If you looked at photos of the men and women in your family tree, would you see ways in which you are like some of them? In my case, I am a writer like my daddy and I am a gardener like my mother. Daddy not only modeled being a writer, but he also encouraged me to think and to research. When I tried to take a shortcut and asked him how to spell a word, he would tell me to get out the dictionary and look it up. I grew up loving dictionaries. My mother modeled being a gardener, and she taught me to work the soil to prepare it for planting. That was before we had tillers, so I learned to turn the soil with a potato fork.

Sometimes we don't realize how important "where we have been" has been to "what we are doing now," and, perhaps, "where we are going." It adds *meaning* to your life to see how, in some ways, you might be continuing in your parents' footsteps. Or, maybe you have reacted by not doing something that your parents did. My parents both smoked cigarettes. I chose not to smoke cigarettes as a young child because I thought it was a waste of money and my mother had a smoker's cough. So, it can work both ways.

Remembering how your ancestors contributed to your values and to your perceptions is like laying a foundation under a house. It's like you are building on the accomplishments of your ancestors and also deciding what mistakes not to repeat. As I thought of this, I remembered that I had previously written about my perceptions when I was a child. I had thought of what was important to me as a young child before I took on responsibilities like making a living.

So, I opened the meeting with what I had written in a self-help workbook. It seems to fit with this chapter, so here we go...

> *When I was a child, I used to think how much fun it would be to ride on a cloud. I envisioned myself sailing along high above the plains of Texas and feeling so free — being carried by a substance that was not really solid and that was capable of changing states — from seemingly solid to liquid spontaneously. It didn't worry me, though, that the cloud beneath me was not solid. I was into the moment. No "What if's" entered my thoughts as a young child yet unfettered by the restrictions and fears constructed by humans. I had not been exposed to "can't" or "impossible." Life seemed full of possibilities." (Laurie Hyatt, Tools for Living: Taking Control of Your Life, 2001).*

So, as we think about stretching ourselves, let's think about these steps to having more expansive thinking:

1. Look at the bigger picture.
2. Be open to "signs" or messages that inspire you
3. What could you do that would be a big challenge?

Have you seen the movie, "Brittany Runs a Marathon"? I saw it today and I felt inspired by the story. The movie is based on a real woman's story. Brittany has been in a rut in her life, and then a series of events serve as catalysts, and she decides to take on a seemingly impossible goal, running the New York City marathon. This is a 28-year-old woman who was very over-weight and out of shape, and had resigned herself to a boring, fairly negative life. She was also carrying some emotional baggage around her parents' divorce. And this woman, who was a naturally gifted comedian, had forgotten, until someone reminded her, that she was also very funny as a child. She had not realized that she was so talented.

Anyway, once she starts taking little steps to losing weight and getting physically fit, she starts to gain self-confidence. Just like life, it's a rocky road, not a smooth path, but that makes achieving success all the more appreciated. Even with many obstacles in her path, she finally achieves her goal, thanks in part to the support of friends, old friends and new friends.

I thought her experiences mirrored life, with its ups and downs, its setbacks and disappointments. But, if, like Brittany, we have visualized the goal, we can eventually persevere and run victoriously over the finish line. **You know what's terrific about the feeling of making something really difficult happen? You feel great!**

ACCOMPLISHING A REALLY DIFFICULT CHALLENGE MAKES YOU FEEL REALLY ALIVE!

What "dream" comes to your mind that, if you turned it into reality, would give you that feeling? Take some time to think about it. For example, have you ever asked yourself, "What would be the perfect way to make money?" The answer is to take what you really enjoy doing and then figure out how to get paid for it. That's how.

There are many ways that you can go about it. One of the ways that we limit ourselves is with "either-or" thinking, either we do this or we do that. Or we do it this way or we do it that way. We tend to think that there are only two choices, because we have been taught this dualistic thinking from our culture. Believe it or not, there are more than two **choices** in how to accomplish something.

I like the story of the guru who had students who came from distant places to learn from his wisdom. One of the exercises that he put them through one day in order to teach them an important concept was to give them a problem to solve. So, the next day, two of the students were called to present their solutions to the problem.

The guru listened intently to the solution posed by the first student. Then he replied, "You're right." Automatically, the second student, raised in an "either-or" way of thinking, thought his solution to the problem must be wrong. But the guru encouraged him to offer his solution. To his amazement, the guru responded, "You're right." They were both perplexed. How could they both be right if they posed different solutions?

Most of us think in terms of right and wrong, either-or. But the wise guru saw the complexities and possibilities of problem-solving. There could be many alternative solutions to the same problem. Both of the students' solutions were correct, even though they were different.

Any time, we have a problem to solve or a plan to devise, we tend to think in this dualistic way. If you're right, then I must be wrong. Or, I can either solve the problem in a certain way, or I am wrong. I know many of you have had the joyous task of helping your children with their math homework. What you may have experienced, like I did, is that teachers often have their own way of teaching how to solve a math problem. You may want to show your child a short-cut or just another way of solving the problem but the well-meaning teacher tells your child that your way is not acceptable. You probably experienced this same dilemma when you were a student.

Other examples of how we limit ourselves with the "either-or" thinking is to tell ourselves, "If I wait to get another college degree, then it won't be possible, because of time or money." I taught psychology classes for the University of Phoenix, where most of the students are working full-time and going to school at night or early in the morning. The classes that I taught were hybrid classes in which the students and I met once a week face-to-face for four hours and the rest of the work was done online. So, older students had the opportunity to go back to college and earn a degree. This is an example of alternative ways to get an education.

How about "If I let too much time go by, then I'll never find a good woman or a good man." False. I had a friend of the family on my mother's side who got married for the first time when she was 79. She was so excited, showing us her new clothes and her wedding dress and telling us her honeymoon plans! So, thinking that either you get married by a certain age or it will not happen is definitely not true. We all make our own path.

If you think about where you have been and what you have experienced, you may realize that what you were exposed to growing up has influenced you more than you realized. You may have been influenced in positive ways or you may still be reacting to some past hurt. I often use the example of separating the wheat from the chaff. In other words, it is best to embrace what has been helpful or useful from your past experiences and let go of the rest.

Also, be grateful for any values and beliefs that you were taught that still define who you are today. Take those and build on that foundation. Discard what is not useful to you now. Add what you have learned or decisions that you have made independently and then ask the question, **"Where do I go from here?"** Literally, where do you want to be living in the future? What occupation would you like to have? What values that you were taught do you want to pass on? What new accomplishments will you add to the story of your heritage?

Chapter 9

Travel Light

As you move forward with your life, it is better to travel light. Get rid of as much heavy baggage as you can. Not only mentally, as this includes people and things. So, I guess what we are doing now is taking an inventory of who and what is in your life. Who propels you forward with encouragement and support and who brings you down somehow? Who or what is distracting you from your path to happiness?

Letting go, especially when it comes to people, can be really difficult, as you probably know all too well. By "letting go," I don't necessarily mean that you are going to no longer associate with them. You might just limit your interactions, especially if the person is a family member. Or maybe you will decrease the amount of time that you waste trying to control them or analyzing their behavior. Also, you could be letting go of people from the past who still occupy too much of your thoughts.

I suggest that you begin by taking some time to list significant people in your life. Now, on paper or in your mind, make two columns, one headed

"Increases my energy" and the other headed **"Depletes my energy."**

Reflect on how each person's current words and actions or past words and actions have taken up your precious energy, either with benefits or with no gain to you. They are like heavy baggage that you are still carrying around for absolutely no rational reason.

HERE'S A STRATEGY
TO HELP YOU LET GO.

Cut or tear some squares of paper. On each one, write who you have decided to let go of and why. I have actually done this. I took some pretty paper and wrote a sentence or two. Then I got some pretty cloth and a ribbon and bundled up the pieces of paper, using the ribbon to tie it up and finish with a bow on top.

Now, burn the bundle or let it go down a river or creek. **Have a ceremony** by yourself or invite a friend or family member to join you. Start a fire in a fire pit or fireplace or find a clear space in your yard where you can safely place the bundle and set it on fire.

As I mentioned, you can also place your bundle in a river or creek and watch it float away until it is out of sight. This reminds me of an episode of the television series, Northern Exposure, from the 90's, season 4, episode 1. In this story, Maggie, who was an airplane pilot and had her own plane, ran a business transporting people and goods to and from a tiny town in Alaska. Anyway, Maggie's 30th birthday was approaching and she decided to celebrate by getting rid of her old baggage. In her case, she wrote letters to all of her old boyfriends, finally writing a goodbye to them so that she would let go of any conflicts and negative feelings that she still harbored.

She rowed a canoe down the river to an isolated area outside of town. When she found a spot that she liked, she set up a tent, and reflected on what she wanted to accomplish. Then, Maggie sent the letters, each in its own envelope, one by one, down the river and waved goodbye to each one. After a long, tiring day, she fell asleep. When she woke up, she realized that she was sick. She had developed a high fever, and began to hallucinate about the boyfriends. In her hallucinations, it was like they were really there all sitting around an outdoor table.

It was really funny what little disagreements that she had let fester in her mind. She had become conflicted about her feelings toward the men. Through this process of writing the letters and then dreaming about the men, she finally saw the relative unimportance of many of the conflicts that she had mulled over in her mind for years.

That episode of Northern Exposure was so

good because many of us watching could relate to her. As I saw her let go of those past relationships, I thought of my own life and the relationships that I had chosen to let go. She had chosen a mile-marker, her 30th birthday, as being an important time in her life to make some changes. She realized that in letting go of the past, she was making room for a happier future.

My experience has been that rituals can be helpful in the letting go process. Having something tangible to actually release helps your mind let go. Now, that thought or idea written on paper is something real that you actually watch disappear.

How about having a ceremony in conjunction with the full moon or the solstice? That might add to the **meaning** behind your ritual. And, now that I'm thinking of it, why not have a ceremony like this once a year, perhaps at the end of December? Or at the end of winter to usher in the new life of spring with a clean slate?

I like to have a yard sale each spring or summer to get rid of all the items that have accumulated in my house and in the houses of neighbors and friends who want to participate. It's actually fun because it turns into a social event, where my neighbors and friends get together and chat while we wait for the next lucky customer to drive up.

Maybe, for you it's the annual trip to Goodwill or another agency that will take what you no longer want and pass it on to someone who does want it. Recycling discarded items is meaningful because you are saving Mother Earth by not throwing everything in a landfill or compactor site and you are adding to someone else's life. There are agencies that take your clothing to help women who are re-entering the work force. Or you can take them to a homeless shelter or a battered women's shelter.

When I worked as a counselor at a battered women's shelter, there were not enough resources and supplies for the women, who often had children with them. People donated toiletries, old cell phones, food, and clothing to women who were in desperate need. Many had left their homes in the middle of the night with just their purse and the clothes on their backs. So, your donation of discarded items is a very meaningful act, helping those in need.

So, we have talked about the various strategies that we can utilize to let go of people and objects in our lives that no longer serve a useful purpose. You can also take your negative feelings for a brisk walk or a run and erase them from your mind as you go. When you are physically working hard, you need all of your energy to get one foot in front of the other. Any extraneous negative thoughts just zap your motivation. So, just tell yourself to let them go so you can have the energy to keep exercising. Also, kind of like Forrest Gump, you can take your conflicted feelings on a run until they are all gone.

Personally, I do some of my best thinking when I'm walking or jogging. Physically taking action can be very cathartic. In times when I have been very upset with someone, I have piled up bathroom towels on the washing machine, and pounded my fist into them as hard as I could. One time, when I was really angry, I let go of the negativity by literally taking a pick ax and thrusting it into the earth over and over to make a bigger pine straw bed around a tree in my yard. So, I was expending a lot of angry energy and also accomplishing something. Screaming out loud really adds to the release, but I guess we have to consider the neighbors.

This sounds silly, but it is a fact that the cells of your body literally hold stress. When you physically exert yourself, you help your physical body let go of the negativity. I once read about a mental hospital that actually took their patients for fast walks or runs instead of prescribing antidepressant medications. The release of endorphins and other chemicals in the body while doing exercise is similar to the effects of medications for some people. The disclaimer here is that some people with a certain body chemistry actually benefit from medication. So, just like the many alternative solutions to a problem that we discussed in the guru story, there are many possible remedies for depressed feelings. Some people experience the relief of symptoms from medication while others can get the same benefit from more physical exercise or a change in a nutritional program.

Whether it's symptoms that you want to eliminate or it's people or things that you choose to let go, the point is to travel light on your life journey. Eliminate people or objects or thoughts that weigh you down or obstruct the view ahead.

One time I read that you cannot attain enlightenment until you have established order in your life. That's pretty profound. **If your goal is to be enlightened, to have greater knowledge and understanding, to have spiritual insight, and to bring Light into your life, it's best to travel light.** To be really happy, to enjoy life, and to have a meaningful life, it makes sense to let go of whatever slows your way forward.

Years ago, when I was working as a mental health counselor, I realized that I would benefit from a mental health break of my own. So, I signed up for a weekend retreat in a mountain cabin. The serenity of a low-key not-too-structured weekend in a mountain cabin with simple meals, morning stretches, and a few group exercises was just what I needed to feel re-vitalized. One of the facilitators was an art therapist. I remember that she gave us a directive to draw something that depicted what life was like for us. I drew a river flowing over rocks. When it came my turn to share, I explained that the purpose of life was like the river, to keep flowing. The water's purpose is to keep moving, so that the water remains fresh and clear and full of life. So, when an obstacle is in the way, the water flows over it or around it or underneath it. If the obstacle succeeds in stopping the water, what happens? The water stagnates. Mosquitoes breed. Fish die.

One of our challenges in life is to transcend the obstacles, to go around or over the rocks of life and keep moving.

It's a great analogy to your life. Don't let the obstacles stop you or slow you down. Figure out a way to keep rushing past them. Keep your energy high and use your power to keep moving. Be confident and trust your inner resources to clear a path.

Chapter 10

Anger Can Be Helpful

Have you ever felt angry because you felt that you were being manipulated or controlled? Or have you felt anger because you were being treated with disrespect? Or maybe you thought you were being lied to or that a "friend" was saying one thing and doing another. I'll bet most of you are going, "Yes!!!" Most of us have felt angry for a number of reasons.

I hope that you no longer allow yourself to be downgraded or abused or jerked around by anyone. I hope you never again get off track because of someone who wants to have power over you. But, don't be too hard on yourself. We have all fallen prey to someone else's tricks. Anger can actually make you aware of the falsehoods and signal an alarm to take action. Your anger can give you helpful information. It's like a signal that your rights have been violated.

THE SPIDER WEB OF DECEPTION

Let me explain the reasons why you can get caught in the spider web of deception before you even notice that you have been trapped. There are a couple of dynamics that are often at play. One of the traps has to do with **the behavior of the person who is disrespecting you** and the other has to do with **your responses to their attempts to pull you down.**

People can fool you because they sneak up on you gradually and because people's complexities can throw you off. Some people can make subtle changes in their behavior over time so that you don't notice that they are manipulating you. For example, a person can be really thoughtful and affectionate at first. Then, when they get you hooked, they make a degrading remark or tell you that you can't dress a certain way. Sometimes, they act jealous, which can be flattering. **You get sucked in by their charm.**

Remember how we talked about jealousy in a previous chapter? Beware of jealousy in others, just like you now know not to be jealous of others. Jealousy is a red flag signaling you that the other person is starting to control you.

Then there is the game where the other person doesn't respond to your phone calls or text messages. Let's say you meet a guy for coffee. This is the first time you have seen him. The conversation is pleasant, maybe he is witty and smart. You are attracted. But he does not contact you again. Just like when we discussed the aloof person and how easy it is to start second guessing why you don't hear from him again. "Should I have worn a more attractive outfit?" "Did I say something offensive?" "Was I boring"? The self-deprecating chatter goes on and on. You know why?

Many of you were raised to be pleasers. You were taught to be kind and thoughtful. In this case, sometimes, your blessing can be your curse. Your tendency to be kind and thoughtful is a blessing, but it can also work against you. Years ago, my daddy gave me a copy of *Autobiography with Letters* (1939) by William Lyon Phelps. During his lifetime, William Lyon Phelps was a well-known author, professor of literature, and critic. Daddy enjoyed the story and also the bits of wisdom in the book. One of the lessons in the book that I resonated with was that **there is a fine line between being kind and being foolish.** This lesson comes back into my consciousness often because I have gone over that fine line so many times myself.

There are so many ways that we get confused and end up being foolish. You might question why your acts of kindness are not reciprocated with respect, for example. You tell yourself that you are inadequate, when the truth is that the other person is self-absorbed. Maybe you think that someone really deserves your help when, in fact, that person is narcissistic. In some cases, the person has a really pitiful story and you feel sympathy, when they are really just manipulating you for their own personal gain. Sometimes people act helpless, and you mistakenly tell yourself, "She doesn't have anyone else." Before you know it, you are doing all the work or paying all the bills, while they do very little in return. Then you start feeling angry. That anger is telling you to make changes, to take action.

Another reason that we can mis-judge a person is that **people are complicated and complex.** The same person who volunteers at the food bank in the morning may rob a store that night. People are multi-faceted. They have many sides, like well-cut diamonds. One side may be helpful to someone in need and the other side of the same person might be abusive to his wife. Many people demonstrate behaviors that are kind and thoughtful one day and the next day act disrespectfully toward the one they profess to love.

This can be very confusing. It can throw us off when we are trying to decide whether to pursue a relationship or to continue a relationship. The disrespectful behavior is often followed by the sweetest gift. Uh, oh! Here we go. Hooked again. Sometimes it seems like Mr. or Miss Wonderful knows just how far to push the envelope to keep you mesmerized. Until you finally get angry and make some changes.

Sometimes we feel like we're on a roller coaster. I remember a time many years ago actually having a dream that I was riding an out of control roller coaster and I couldn't get off. When I woke up, I was exhausted and frustrated.

I have seen videos by marriage counselors where they tell spouses that when the negative remarks to each other outnumber the positive remarks, the marriage is in trouble. The marriage is in even worse peril if the negative remarks are bitterly hostile. I would certainly agree.

It is common in communication skills training sessions to suggest that you preface a criticism with an acknowledgement of a job well done. An example of this might be, "I really appreciate you going to the store, but next time remember the milk." That sounds good on paper, as they say, but it's not real life. If you have to remember the rules of politeness every time you want to make a point to a significant other, the whole thing seems rigid.

But the general principle of weighing the negative and the positive could be helpful. After all, we all have times when we are not at our best and we say something that we wish we hadn't or we don't say something that we wish we had. In all the messiness of relationship and communication, I think that the most important strategy is honesty. Just say out loud what your mind is thinking. Have you ever thought of how your life would be different if you didn't gloss over your thoughts and just said what was on your mind? It would be so freeing, wouldn't it?

Sometimes the confusion comes from the contrast between someone's words and their actions like the old saying, "Say one thing and do another." They say, "I really like you" and then they disappear. Or they say, "I care about you so much," and then disregard something really important to you.

REFLECTING ON YOUR ANGER IS A HELPFUL STRATEGY

Did you think I had forgotten about anger as a strategy? That was a long lead-in, but I'm inserting here that the strategy that you can pull out of your hat is to let your feelings of anger inform you. Some people think that it is better not to feel angry. They think that anger should be suppressed. Greet the world with "I'm fine" even when you don't feel fine at all. We are taught to be pleasant even when we are really distressed. That's the script that we are supposed to read.

I don't think so. I suggest that you get more aware of your feelings of anger and use them to decide your next course of action. **Your anger can tell you that your rights are being violated.** Pay attention to your angry feelings. Trust yourself. When you feel angry, there is probably a good reason. Don't sweep your anger under the rug. Look at it. Be with it. Stay with the angry feelings for at least ten minutes. And then see what occurs to you.

Here's a little exercise to make the point. I want you to feel angry right now. Take all the time you need to get angry. Let your body feel angry, maybe breathing faster than usual, maybe feeling flushed, maybe your heart is beating fast.

Now, how did you do that? How did you create those angry feelings? Ah, ha! You *thought about* a time when you were really angry. Someone had been unfair. Someone had humiliated you in front of your co-workers. Someone had ignored who you are. Or even worse. The point is that you created those feelings of anger with your thoughts.

Trust that you might have really been treated unfairly. Trust that anyone who was in a similar situation of being humiliated in front of their co-workers would be angry. I remember one time many years ago, I worked in a job titled "Behavior Specialist" with a population who was intellectually challenged, some very severely. It was lunch time and I was working with clients who were severely challenged in a building detached from the main sheltered workshop. One of the clients was eating grapes and accidentally swallowed the stem and began to choke. When she turned blue and the regular Heimlich maneuver didn't work, my colleague and I decided that we would have to do the procedure of last resort, literally reach down the client's throat and grab the stem and pull it out of her throat. It worked, the stem was retrieved, and the client immediately breathed and was fine.

When I got back to the main building, the

Director criticized me in front of my co-workers, telling me that I had not followed procedure. I explained that we went through the necessary steps. And, I added, the client is alive because of the steps that we took. When she kept putting me down, I was furious. It wasn't long before I began looking for a different job.

Angry feelings can alert you that change is needed. Maybe just being more assertive and speaking your mind is all that is needed to come to an understanding. But, sometimes, when that doesn't get the desired result, a bigger change would be better.

I don't get angry very often. Frankly, I don't like the uncomfortable feelings that come along with feeling angry. But I know that when I feel angry, there is a usually a reason. An exception would be if I misunderstood what was said or I really didn't know the context of a situation. Then I might feel angry for no real reason. But, for the most part, anger is your friend.

Because we have been taught not to make waves, we sometimes let ourselves cool off until the angry feelings dissipate and then we tell ourselves, "It was no big deal" or "I'm over-reacting" or "I was just tired and stressed out." We disregard our own feelings. And often we hang onto bitterness and resentment. We carry that baggage around instead of addressing the issue.

One way to help yourself decide if your angry feelings have merit is to share your experience with a trusted friend or family member. Someone who can be objective. See what they think. Does your friend or relative think your feelings of anger were justified? What would they do if they were in your place? I'm not saying to value their opinion over yours. I just think that a "second opinion" might help you clarify your thinking. It's like having a "sounding board." Someone to bounce things off of before **you** decide what to say or do.

Here are some questions for you...

1. When have you felt angry recently?
2. What was the issue?
3. What did you do or not do?
4. Do you still feel angry or upset about that situation?
5. What could you do to resolve your angry feelings?

Chapter 11

Energy

Each of us is an energy field. We produce energy to maintain our bodies, to keep our minds sharp, and to be resilient. Our discussion of anger focused on how we can use anger to detect something that is threatening to take our energy, to deplete our store of energy, to interfere with our natural ability to be productive and happy.

When I am planning my spring garden, I buy lots of seeds to plant in my 30' by 50' fenced in area. I grow Better Boy tomatoes, which are about 5' tall when fully grown and are so heavy with big, juicy tomatoes that they have to be staked or caged to keep them from falling over. I also grow green beans that climb the six- foot fence. I grow bell peppers and hot peppers. Did you know that you have to grow bell peppers and hot peppers in separate areas of your garden because the hot peppers will flavor the bell peppers if they are in close range? The energy of the hot pepper plants transfers to the bell pepper plants.

I plant seeds in my greenhouse and then transfer the plants with 4 or 5 leaves to the garden when it is warm enough. The reason that I grow a garden is to feed my family, my neighbors, and my friends. And, frankly, I sell some to make money. The seeds grow into plants that produce vegetables that nourish and give energy. I also garden because it's fun and it energizes me.

MAINTAINING AND INCREASING ENERGY TAKES WORK

But I can't just plant the garden and then forget it for 70 to 90 days and think the plants will fend for themselves. Growing a healthy garden requires **strategy, planning, and tools** to turn the soil and rid the ground of pesky weeds. In *Think Your Way to Happiness* I give you **strategies and tools** to use so that you can be as happy as I am and have joyful, meaningful lives.

So, just as I draw out my garden plan, put seeds in little containers and then when they are strong enough I dig holes and plant them in the garden, **you can re-imagine your life and decide what thoughts and ideas and people to keep in your energy sphere and nurture.** When I garden, I use a potato fork and Larry pushes a tiller to churn the soil and mix in nutrients like compost ingredients from the kitchen and fertilizer and sometimes lime. These ingredients add to the life force of the plants, giving them energy to produce the results that I want.

I use a hoe to get rid of weeds that will deprive

my vegetables of energy and nourishment. They suck up the vital water and nutrients from the soil. They are stealing nutrition from my tomatoes, green beans, and peppers. And, you know what, weeds don't add joy to my life. As far as I am concerned, weeds are just depriving my potentially producing plants from getting the nutrition, and in some cases, sunshine, that they need in order to grow and produce.

The weeds are examples of obstacles in our way or people who drain us and things that don't serve a meaningful purpose in our lives. So, I choose to use my hoe and my hands to tear out and pull up the weeds that are draining the energy from the productive plants. They are using up resources that my tomatoes depend on to grow tall and produce bread-size tomatoes for those yummy tomato sandwiches. I see it as my responsibility to rid the garden of anything that stands in the way of my vegetable producers getting the water, nutrients, fresh air, and sunshine that vitalize them, that give them the energy to burst through the earth and grow higher and fuller.

You know, it's hard work to keep all the critters from harming my vegetables, too. We have a 6' fence to keep the deer out. Much as I love to see the beautiful deer grazing on grass in the far side of the yard, I am not willing to share my garden with them. Let me see, there has to be a good analogy here. I know. You can care about someone without choosing to take care of them. How about that! I care about the deer, but I'm not going to take care of them.

Birds can also be annoying when they swoop down and gouge holes in my ripe tomatoes. So, we have a fake owl and a scarecrow and tin pans waving on the ends of strings. And don't forget bugs and worms and slugs and snails. I'm sure that Japanese beetles have a purpose in God's plan, but not on my green beans. So many creatures that can potentially destroy my harvest. I am constantly vigilant, checking my plants for evidence of energy stealers and promptly getting rid of them.

Plants can't be too close together, either, or they won't get enough fresh air and sunshine. I was ecstatic a few weeks ago when I found seeds for sale to grow mammoth sunflowers that actually have seeds big enough to roast and eat. They grow to be 7' to 12' tall. Years ago, when I lived in a Marietta, Georgia, my neighbor and I had a contest to see who could grow the tallest sunflowers. He won. More sun, I guess. You have to provide a big space between these huge sunflower plants so they can get full sun all day. It's the same with us. We need energy all day.

It is best to rid our lives of people and activities that steal our energy. **It is also best to have personal space to think and reflect and have some alone time to fill up our energy reservoir again.**

Have you ever noticed that if another person stands too close to you, that you will automatically step back? In our American culture, the space is about 12". If someone gets closer than that, unless you are in a crowded train at the airport or in a crowded subway or a similar situation, you will step away.

Anyway, whatever the culture and whatever the specific measured space, we all need our own personal space. Have you ever heard someone say, "She was suffocating me" or "I just needed to get away for a while?" There you go. **Like my giant sunflowers, we need space.**

While I am thinking of sunflowers, do you know how sunflowers got their name? Because they literally follow the sun all day. They lean toward the east in the morning and throughout the day, they turn westward toward the setting sun. Sunflowers lock in on their energy source, the sun. They literally follow their energy source all day. To me, this is a powerful example of how nature can be a good model for us. What if we followed our energy source all day instead of letting obstacles get in the way or getting distracted by unimportant matters?

We all generate energy in order to survive and to thrive.

Take some time to answer these questions:

1. How do you generate physical, mental, and emotional energy?
2. What is the source of your energy?
3. What drains your energy? This could be people, activities, places.
4. Which people in your life energize you? What activities make you feel more energetic? Are there certain places in the United States or in your city or specifically where you live that increase your energy?

You may not have ever thought of yourself as a field of energy. You are constantly generating more energy. Everyone has their own field of energy. If someone is chronically depressed, they don't have as much energy as someone who is happy, for example. And, on the other hand, some people have so much energy that they emit energy outward and you may benefit from their overstock.

Today, I was walking at our local Lakeshore Mall in Gainesville, Georgia, and I had the lucky experience of benefitting from a stranger's energy. I was walking toward a young man in his early 20's when he looked right at me with a very warm, almost knowing, smile. I, of course, responded with a smile. But what jolted me was that as I passed him, I got chill bumps and a "high" feeling that lasted for several minutes. I had entered his energy field and it felt great.

Richard Simmons, the exercise guru, used to say, "Surround yourself with positive people." Thank you, Richard, for the wise advice. I'll interject here for fun that I was selected to be in one of Richard's commercials years ago. I participated in aerobics classes at one of his Anatomy Asylum exercise clubs. Before class one day I completed a sentence on a questionnaire that read, "I love Anatomy Asylum because…" My response got me in the top 50 contestants vying to participate in a television commercial with him. The next step was to be filmed in Atlanta sharing why I loved Anatomy Asylum and how it had helped me. I ended my two-minute segment with "Working out at Anatomy Asylum is something I do just for me." This was not original. Richard used to stress the importance of doing something just for yourself.

Anyway, Richard selected me and 11 others from all over the United States to be in his commercial based on our videos. He paid to fly us all out to Detroit and also provided really nice hotel rooms and meals. When we got to Detroit, he spent time with each of us, watched our videos with each of us individually, and explained why he chose us. He said to me, "Laurie, I chose you because you said that Anatomy Asylum was something you did just for yourself."

Richard Simmons focused his attention and energy on each of us because he really cared about our well-being. The experience is one that I obviously have never forgotten. Richard had so much energy to give and he gave with enthusiasm and sincerity. Actually, he is still inspiring us to be our best selves. He has a new wall calendar "Richard Simmons 2020" that can motivate you for the new year.

A couple of weeks after I got home, there was a personal note to me from Richard in my mailbox. "Didn't we have fun!" he exclaimed. And guess what else he did?! He would just show up at my local Anatomy Asylum, as he did at all the Anatomy Asylums, unannounced and lead our exercise class. And, are you ready for this…he asked about my children that were in the Anatomy Asylum child care center and said, "Let's go see them!" And he did. Richard exuded intense, warm, genuine energy.

When you are fortunate enough to interact with a positive energy source, be grateful and soak it in. There are so many people out there whose intention is to steal your energy. I hope that, for the most part, you can avoid them or at least limit your time with them.

Send a message out to the universe to bring more positive people into your life. Be open to opportunities to spend time with highly energetic people. Concentrate on your clear intention to increase your emotional, mental, and physical energy.

Be grateful for the highly energetic people that you are fortunate enough to meet. Soak in their positive vibes and whisper, "Thank you!" to the universe. Increase your energy by sending out positive thoughts, believe that they will be received, and, like a boomerang, more energy will come your way.

Chapter 12

Increasing Your Personal Power

Now that you have a clear intention to rid your life of people and activities that steal your energy, what are other ways that you can actually increase your energy? In other words, how do you increase your personal power? First, you nurture and nourish yourself. Then you get balanced and centered. And third, you fill yourself up with inspiration and focus on the highest idea of yourself.

You may be surprised that I am talking about literally nourishing and nurturing your physical body in a book about thinking your way to happiness. Well, of course I am. **One of the important contributors to my ability to generate happy thoughts and to feel joy and create meaning in my life is my physical fitness.** Yes, I'm serious.

When I wake up in the morning, I feel energetic, thanks to the effort I make to be physically healthy…and, okay, thanks to a cup of strong coffee, too. I am no stranger to exercise and counting vegetables consumed. It takes lots of energy to turn your dreams into reality. Here's the way I look at life.

I BELIEVE THAT
WE ARE ALL SPIRITUAL
BEINGS IN A HUMAN BODY.

The body and the spirit work together to produce energy. So, eating nutritious foods produces fuel that converts to energy. I suggest that you make yourself a food tracker where you literally write down what you eat and count the 5 fruits and vegetables you eat each day. And be sure to drink about 8 cups of water a day, too. For my personal tracker, I made headings for breakfast, lunch, and dinner, and I make a line for water with numbers beside. I included a facsimile at the end of this book. I print about 30 copies at a time and insert them in a 3-ring binder, titled, "I'm healthy!" Many of you will probably download your tracker in your phone.

Begin by checking out the nutrition on food labels. If you haven't made a habit of this, you will be amazed at the junk in some foods. Yogurt is a great example. The healthy brand that I bought last week has the following ingredients: "cultured pasteurized organic nonfat milk" and "5 live active cultures." That's all. Some of the other brands at the same grocery store have 6 or 8 ingredients. I'm not kidding. A bunch of chemicals.

Here's another one. Look at different types of chocolate. See if you can find a chocolate where the ingredient listed first is cocoa instead of sugar. It has more antioxidants. Oh, how about those little containers of applesauce. You can find them with or without corn syrup. The natural applesauce tastes better and it's loaded with nutrients which convert to energy.

You won't believe what I'm snacking on while I write to you. Steamed broccoli with a dab of melted butter. Oh, my gosh, it is so good! Take some time to think about what you are eating that fuels your body.

I have to say that I am not a fanatic. I like sweets and I eat them. I just made a batch of chocolate chip cookies yesterday. So, I'm talking about moderation and balance, not extremes. To be honest, you want to create a food plan that you can really live with and enjoy. Remember that I suggested at the beginning of this book that you change your thinking and your actions about 80% of the time? So, how about eating healthy about 80% of the time? For example, if you eat 2,000 calories a day to maintain your weight, reserve at least 400 calories for something fun, like dessert.

I focus on what I am adding to my food choices, not what I'm taking away. Adding lots of fruits and vegetables and plenty of water is my most important consideration.

Schedule some exercise most days. If you are already an exerciser like I am, you may just want to maintain what you're doing or change it up a bit once in a while to make it interesting. If you haven't been doing much exercise, I hope you schedule exercise on your calendar just like you schedule your other activities.

No matter where you are with your exercise program, you might add steps every week or add weights just to keep yourself challenged. I often get sidetracked over the holidays, but then I get back to walking 10,000 steps, which is about 4.25 miles for my step length, 4 or 5 days a week. We have an indoor shopping mall close to my house, so I can walk there with my walking buddy, Barbara, even when it's raining outside. In the spring, I'll add some jogging, but I won't increase the distance. The goal is to increase your stamina. When your heart is pumping faster and you're breathing a little deeper and you're building muscles, that's increasing your body's energy level.

If you don't already own one, I really suggest that you buy a Fitbit or Apple watch. There are also lots of free apps on your smart phone. My Fitbit is like my coach or my cheerleader. When I walk my 10,000 steps, the Fitbit vibrates and I see a visual image of fireworks on the screen. Throughout the day, it nudges me to walk a little. "How about 129 steps in the next 10 minutes," shows up on the screen and other little goals and when I complete that, it will go "Easy peazy!" It makes exercise a lot more fun.

So, get moving. Once your body is moving, it seems more natural to take action on other goals. You've got some inertia going. And once you accomplish a few small goals, you are on a roll.

I like the way I feel when I get into a routine of exercise. And I know it's easy to get off track and hard to get back into scheduling time for yourself.

Intellectually, you can energize yourself by reading books that challenge you to think. I have included a few of my favorite books at the end of this book. You can also attend workshops, classes, conferences, and retreats. You can even have deep conversations that feed your brain.

Emotionally, you can fill yourself up by expressing your feelings, thoughts, and concerns to someone who really listens to you. I want to emphasize that not everyone is a good listener, and that is all right. Don't waste your energy criticizing the ones who don't listen. In fact, some people are "doer's" and not listeners, just as some people learn by reading and some learn by hands-on activity. So, spend your time finding people who listen well. That's one reason that I started women's personal growth groups. I knew that the women who participated would, for the most part, be good listeners.

Spiritually, you create more personal power by spending time with the Creator, spending time in a sacred space or power place, having quiet time, being in Nature. If the idea of a power place or a sacred space is new to you, I'll explain. I really don't know if the power or sacredness is innate to the place or to your experience of the space. Let me give you an example. When I lived in the north Georgia mountains in a little log cabin, I walked the dirt roads frequently. I noticed that I was drawn to some specific places more than others.

Actually, I have a funny story to tell you before I explain what a power place is. On my first walk through Walnut Mountain, I heard birds singing loudly. I stopped and listened in wonder. I really thought that the developers had piped in bird calls to add to the ambiance! Then I caught myself and realized that I was really in the mountains where many kinds of birds live. Real birds were really singing and talking with each other. There was life everywhere!

Now, back to the power place explanation. So, I walked on for quite a while until I came upon a piece of property where a house had been and only a chimney remained. There was no evidence of what had happened to the house, maybe a fire or a big storm had taken it down. But I got chill bumps when I approached. I almost felt like crying. I definitely felt energy. You could have many explanations for what I experienced in that space. Maybe I was connecting with the spirits of people who had lived there. I don't know. I do know that over the years, every time I was close to that space, I felt a strong vibration.

Try this exercise. Go out in your yard and walk very slowly, being very aware of your surroundings. Notice how you feel in different areas. If you really pay attention, there are areas of your yard that you just plainly like better than others. You like being there more. You almost feel a smile on your face in that spot or you just feel comfortable there. Maybe you are drawn to a spot where you just want to grab a chair and sit there for a while. Maybe the view there is pretty or there is a tree that speaks to you. Focus on your footsteps. Do your feet just want to stop and back up and walk over that space again? That is one of your power places.

If you live in an apartment and you don't have a yard, then walk or drive to a park or a common area or wherever you can in Nature. Practice this exercise with an open mind until your heightened awareness tips you off to a place that feels special to you. If you have ever been to Sedona, Arizona, you probably know that people travel there from all over the world because of the energy vortices. Read up on it. Apparently, the geology of the earth in that part of the world has components that radiate various kinds of energy. Tours of Sedona usually include a stop at an energy vortex.

Okay, here's another example. Has anyone ever given you a gem or stone or crystal for a particular reason? When my son died, a Navajo friend gave me a crystal to hold tightly in the palm of my hand to give me strength. My friend, Iris

Bolton, author of the book, *My son, My son,* and an inspiring speaker, often provides stones at speaking engagements with instructions to pick one to take home. Different stones will give you different energies, depending on the individual person. My daughter, Heather, brought me a polished stone from her travels that is intended to energize my creativity for writing. I have it right here beside my computer.

You know that in our culture, we love superheroes. They have immense personal power, both physical power and mental and emotional power. We love superheroes because we dream of having super powers ourselves. How life would be better if we could overcome the enemy or eliminate the evil force. When iron man put on his suit, you knew that he was going to be able to do many feats that he couldn't do without the suit. The Iron Man suit gave him power.

We don't literally have a superhero suit, but we do have a lot of strategies to increase our personal power. We can change the way we think from self-defeating thoughts to self-confident thoughts that leave no room for doubt. We can see ourselves as important, with a mission that motivates us to take action. We can increase our physical power with nutritious foods and exercise. We can develop our spirituality by spending time communicating with our Creator, asking for inspiration and guidance or meditating for mindfulness.

There are many ways to increase your personal power.

1. How do you manifest personal power right now?
2. What can you do to increase your personal power?
3. What can you start doing today to heighten your awareness of your own personal power and the personal power of others?

Chapter 13

What Do You Believe?

A meaningful life comes from the belief that you have a purpose. To be happy, it is important to believe that life is meaningful. When you have a positive outlook, you know that life itself, and your life in particular, are purposeful and significant. When you have a meaningful life, you take actions that are based on your knowledge of what direction you are going and why.

THERE ARE MANY BELIEFS ABOUT WHAT GIVES LIFE MEANING.

Some of you may have religious beliefs that give your life direction and purpose. Some of you may believe that there is a life force that you attribute to creating all life, but you don't subscribe to a particular religion or religious denomination. Or you may find meaning in taking care of Mother Earth and the life forms that inhabit the earth by sustaining the environment. Still others find purpose and meaning in family, raising children and helping family members.

When I worked as a mental health counselor on the Hopi Reservation, I was inspired by an existential question in a framed wall hanging over a Hopi social worker's desk. It read, **"What difference did you make today?"** Making a positive difference, in whatever form, means that you have served a purpose that day. You have contributed to the greater good.

I think that it is a bit confusing to young people when they consider all the various beliefs about how life was created and how life is sustained. Young people are often struggling to figure out for themselves what gives their life meaning and purpose. My hope is that as we all determine what is meaningful to us, that we also honor what is meaningful to others.

While acknowledging that there are many beliefs concerning how we got here and why, I would like to focus on the obvious. You and I are humans living on a planet that is spinning through a huge and constantly expanding space. You are one of about 7.8 billion human beings living on planet Earth. The earth has oceans and mountains and forests. Other life forms that we share the planet with include trees and other plants, animals, creatures of the seas, rivers, and lakes. We have air to breathe, sunshine, water, and various food sources. Each year, more planets are discovered in vast outer space and more creatures are discovered in the depths of the oceans.

I encourage you to ponder all of the mysteries

of life with a child's sense of wonder and awe. Don't take it for granted. Be thankful when a golden full moon takes your breath away or a bright pink and yellow sunset leaves you spellbound. Spend time in Nature. I suggest that you set a goal for yourself to spend time outdoors as much as possible. If you are reading a book and it's a warm day, take the book outside.

Really experience Nature. When you devote time as often as you can to going outside and just observing the birds and the plants and butterflies, it is obvious that there is a life plan. There is order to what is going on. Bees are pollinating. Animals are procreating. Worms are aerating the dirt. All of the activity is entertaining and fun to watch. **As you feel more and more a part of the life cycle, it will become apparent to you that you are also a vital part of the action.**

You will know that your life has meaning and purpose, just as it is apparent that all the plants and creatures have a purpose. To keep life going. To contribute to the cycle of life. To play a part in the growth and health of everything around us.

When you become aware of the sacredness of life, you will be motivated to align yourself with the life energy, like the sunflowers do. You will create your own path, your own destiny, utilizing your individual beliefs, talents, and interests.

BE OPEN TO EXPERIENCE.

Put aside everything that limits you and spend more time with everything that fills you up. Take time to be still and listen and watch. We get so busy doing, doing, doing that we don't take enough time to just be. See yourself, literally and figuratively, like a vessel of water that needs to be filled up again every day after the contents have been emptied.

You know that all the busyness of life can get us off course. We can easily forget what is really important. We can neglect our spiritual self. It takes so much energy just to meet survival requirements like work or school and paying bills and doing laundry and buying food. Many of us also spend a lot of energy helping others, which is part of our purpose. All of this activity is necessary. What is important is to also carve out time to be still. To listen. To receive inspiration and guidance. To see ourselves as part of something much bigger.

Begin to believe that you play an essential role in a bigger energy field and that there are energy sources all around you. Each of us generates energy, too. We are walking, talking energizers. We generate our own energy.

WHAT DO YOU BELIEVE IS IMPORTANT? THESE STRATEGIES WILL GET YOU STARTED.

1. Developing life-affirming beliefs about yourself and the world around you.
2. Creating your own life path and not comparing your life journey to others.
3. Being true to your own values.
4. Spending time making a difference in your own ways.
5. Spending time developing your highest idea of yourself.

You can add more specific beliefs to these from your own perspective. How do you believe you can best spend your time? What do you believe you have to contribute? Do you have some specific beliefs that determine how you think and what actions you choose to take?

What you believe makes all the difference in what you think about and how you feel and what you choose to do. When you believe that you can move up the ladder in your career, then you probably will. When you believe that you can create a fulfilling, satisfying life with or without a "significant other," then you will find contentment. When you believe that you can let go of whatever is draining your energy and find new people or activities that will lift you up, then those people and activities will materialize.

When you believe that you can start your own business doing what you love to do, then you can make it happen. When you believe, like I did, that you are smart enough and persistent enough to go back to school at any age and get another degree or technical skill, then you will. Based on that firm belief, you will do the necessary research to find a program and teachers that are a good fit for your goals and your personality.

When you believe that you can go back to work at any age to supplement your income or pay off some nagging bills or renovate your home, then you will look at the opportunities, apply, and get out there and make it happen. When you believe that you can have the lifestyle of your dreams, then you will learn from those who have already accomplished that goal.

When, not if, you believe that you can sell your home of 30 years and move to another state to be closer to family members, then you will get help to do what is necessary to make that happen. My mother, at age 65, sold the Texas house that she and Daddy had lived in for 25 years and moved to Georgia to be closer to me and my family. When I look back, I am really impressed with her because my Daddy was not well, she never drove a car so she was not as mobile as I am, and I could only be helpful remotely because I was raising children in Georgia.

How about people with all kinds of challenges who believe they can compete in a race on foot or in a wheelchair? What about artists who were born with no hands and paint with their feet? What about a young child who collects and distributes warm coats to those who are homeless? **I know you can think of so many more inspiring stories of fellow human beings who believed that they could achieve important goals and they did.**

1. What do you believe are your individual strengths?
2. What do you believe is your role in the bigger picture of life?
3. What do you believe you have done to make someone else's life easier?
4. What would you do if you believed without a doubt that you could achieve it?

Chapter 14

Perfection Is Not A Goal

Here's a fun quote from the actress and comedian, Mae West, that exemplifies my next point:

> *"I generally avoid temptation unless I can't resist it."*

We all have given into temptation, whether it's eating that piece of cake that was not on our weight loss plan or going on a date with someone that you knew wasn't "good for you." Many of us, certainly including me, have made mistakes that had serious consequences. And some of us have hung on to guilt and feelings of shame. Just know that if you are human, you have made mistakes. You are not perfect and you will not ever be perfect. No one is. So, perfection is not a life goal. We are all still learning.

You may have blamed yourself for a misjudgment or for not taking action in a situation that was leading to a negative outcome. You may have assessed your children's or your spouse's circumstances and told yourself, "If I had done this…" or "If I had done that…" then they would have acted differently. Or, "If I had stopped my spouse from doing that" or "Why didn't I see what was really going on?"

The list of potential fault-finding statements could go on and on. I could fill pages with them. Most of us have blamed ourselves or blamed our parents or blamed our spouse for a boat load of mistakes. And where did it get us? Unhappy, that's for sure. Miserable, probably. Feeling guilty---check.

Most of you have had preconceived ideas about people or situations. Our assessments were sometimes inaccurate. "If only I had…" can wedge you into a corner that traps you into obsessing over and over about "What if I had…" You wish you could turn back time.

IF YOU ARE HUMAN AND YOU HAVE HAD EXPERIENCES INTERACTING WITH OTHER HUMANS, THEN YOU HAVE MADE MISTAKES IN JUDGMENT.

Either you got into a relationship that turned out to be toxic or you stayed in a toxic relationship way past the point of no return. Maybe you gave someone the benefit of the doubt about a dozen times too many. I certainly have. Or maybe you didn't think the lack of values in a lost soul would make a difference in your relationship and were shocked when their disrespect toward you felt like a slap in the face.

"If only…" "If only…" "If only…" It can be an almost bottomless rut that is hard to get out of.

Here's a good place for a story, which is not original to me, so you may have heard it before.

A man walks down the street. He doesn't see a deep hole in the asphalt, and he falls in.

The next day, the same man walks down the same street. He remembers the deep hole just in time to swerve around it and keep himself from falling in again.

The third day, the same man walks down a different street.

It takes life experience and reflection to learn to make different choices, especially when it comes to choosing an entirely different path. Here's an important tool: **Let go of guilt.** Guilt is heavy and suffocating. Guilt is personal. Guilt infers that there is something wrong with you. So, don't feel guilty.

A better choice is regret. We all have regrets. Regret suggests that you took an action or said something that you wish you hadn't. Regret is about a behavior that you chose at the time, with the information you had or the life situation that you were in at the time. Regret is a product of an error in judgment. Remember that you are a human being. Allow yourself to be human, which means that you will make mistakes. You are still loved…by God, yourself, and others. You are still capable of making terrific decisions in the future. Regret is not about you personally. It is about a course of action that you chose at a particular time in your life.

We are all slow learners at times. Many of us ignore the well-meaning admonitions of friends who suggest to you, "She's just using you" or "He's taking advantage of you." Sometimes we want to help someone who refuses our help or takes our money without a "thank you" or uses up our time and energy and then turns around and blames us for their problems.

Even now, with all my years of personal and professional experience relating to human behavior, I am amazed at how narcissistic some people can be. Or how quickly someone can deny responsibility for their words or actions and, instead, deflect to someone else.

In 1964, a great little book was published called *Games People Play*. The author, Eric Berne, described many disingenuous mind games that people play that still hook many of us today. One was "If it weren't for you, I" in which the manipulator blames all of his or her misfortunes on the other guy.

Don't fall for this destructive game. When you have made many attempts to help someone, with your time and attention or your money, and their behavior continues to be detrimental to you, to themselves, or to others and, shockingly, they blame you for their problems, it is time to cut them loose. As hard as it is for some of us idealistic souls to accept, you cannot save everyone.

Sometimes it's best to let go, to walk away, to delete them from your contact list. Don't feel guilty about your own indiscretions and don't take the blame for the indiscretions of others. Don't burden your soul with guilt from your past and don't blame yourself for the actions of others.

This is a good place to emphasize the importance of taking time for reflection. In the story about the man encountering a deep hole as he walked down the street, you might have noticed a big change from his behaviors on days one and two and his behavior on day three. He apparently took some time to reflect on his dilemma after his experience on day two. He almost fell in the hole again on day two, so he must have pushed "pause" to take time to reflect on what happened. Then, on day three, he had made the decision to take an entirely different route.

He didn't spend days beating himself up for initially falling in the hole and then almost falling in the hole again. Instead, he focused on possible solutions. This is an obvious analogy to our lives. His choice of a different street could be your choice of a different job or a different friend or just choosing an alternative solution to any of a number of problems.

Remember, you are not perfect. You will make mistakes. No one is perfect.

Traditional Navajo women sometimes skip a

thread on purpose when they weave a blanket.
Why? The Navajo women, in their wisdom, are acknowledging the imperfections of life, of the human condition. They do not expect perfection. They do not plan for perfection. They know that their blanket is beautiful with its flaws. You are, too.

WHEN YOU HAVE REALISTIC EXPECTATIONS FOR YOURSELF, YOU CAN ACHIEVE PEACE OF MIND.

You can feel contentment with whatever you do. Enjoy the accomplishment of making a cake that tastes delicious, even if you ran out of icing before covering the sides. Feel great when you wear a skirt that is attractive and fits well, even if a seam isn't quite straight.

When I got married the first time, I was head over heels with the idea of sewing my own wedding gown, even though I had never taken on that intricate a project. When I was sewing a dart on the hipline of the front of the satin dress, I got it an inch or so off the mark. Luckily, I took a deep breath and just decided to add more lace to the front of the dress, which covered my mistake and actually made the dress look even prettier. I know, sometimes mistakes can't be covered. They just have to be accepted as part of our imperfect humanness.

So, we have talked about several points.

1. No one is perfect.
2. We all make mistakes, so don't obsess on them.
3. Acknowledge and accept your imperfect humanness.
4. You can learn from some of your mistakes.
5. You can change course.

On this last point, I guess you know that "post-it's" were created from a mistake. The little stacks of paper were originally supposed to adhere permanently to each other, but the glue wasn't strong enough. Dr. Spencer Silver, a scientist at 3M, was disappointed when the pages would tear away from each other. It wasn't until years later that a colleague, Art Frye, used a post-it for a book mark in his hymn book and the "post-it" became indispensable. Now, there's an example of a product created from a "mistake" ending up making millions of dollars for the company.

Your goal in life is not to attain perfection. And don't think that you have to be perfect or that circumstances have to be whatever you define as perfect, for you to be happy. Perfectionism can cause great misery, whether you were conditioned by your parents as a child that only perfection, like straight A's, was acceptable, or you put that burden of the expectation of perfection on yourself.

I'll close this chapter with a way to think differently about mistakes. Ask yourself the question, "What would I advise a person that I really love, like my child or my best friend, to tell themselves when they make mistakes?" You would say "Let it go. Nobody's perfect."

Chapter 15

Setting Goals

The best way to set goals is a bit counter-intuitive. You might think that you would start with your goals for today, then goals for the week, the month, the year, five years. But that approach will get you bogged down in the details of your everyday life. "Go to the grocery store." "Get the oil changed in the truck." "Finish the paper for American history class."

START WITH THE LONGEST-RANGE GOAL, THE BIG DREAM.

Some people are fortunate enough to know what future career they are going to pursue when they are in elementary school. But I think most of us just took it day to day in our younger years until we were exposed to ideas that connected with us. Keep in mind, though, that dreams and long-range goals include more than career aspirations. We're talking about all kinds of dreams.

You may dream of saving the environment. Or reducing the number of people living in poverty. Or inventing a new technological device that changes the way people communicate. Or a new computer game. Or playing in a successful musical group that tours the world. Or being one of the astronauts to land on Mars.

Maybe your dreams aren't all tangible. You may want to feel closer to God, or whatever you call the higher power that created and sustains life. You may be searching for the meaning in your life. One of your big goals may be to find peace of mind. Maybe you just want to figure out how to be happy, which is why you are reading this book.

JOURNALING IS A STRATEGY THAT CAN HELP YOU TO ARTICULATE YOUR BIG DREAMS.

You don't have to spend a lot of money on your journal. You can buy a spiral notebook or put paper in a three-ring binder. Whatever you choose for writing your thoughts about your goals, you might start by completing these statements. This will help you get started.

1. I want….
2. I dream about…
3. If I had a million dollars, I would….
4. It is really important to me to….
5. My life would be more meaningful if…
6. My life's purpose is to…
7. What really fascinates me is…
8. The goal that is the best expression of who I am is…

Write about your dreams with no self-imposed limits. And don't use the word "try" because that word is disempowering. I want you to believe that you can achieve your goal. Instead of saying, "I'm going to try to run a 5K race," say, "I'm going to run a 5K race." Start with the biggest dream, the longest-range goal and then follow that by listing your short-range goals.

SETTING MY SHORT-RANGE GOAL OF GETTING MY MOTORCYCLE LICENSE

I thought that telling you about one of my short-range goals, getting a motorcycle license, might be a fun way to help you get started. I decided to get my own motorcycle license because I got tired of waiting for a man to take me for a ride. I liked riding motorcycles and I wanted to ride when I wanted to ride.

So, next, I had to figure out how to go about it. I found a course that included what I needed to know to pass the written test and the skills that I needed to pass the driving test. The course included actually taking the written test and the driving test, so, when I finished the course, I could get the motorcycle designation added to my driver's license.

I signed up for a four-day class in Alpharetta, Georgia. Each day, I watched videos, listened to lectures, and spent hours riding a 175-horsepower motorcycle according to the instructor's directions. I was in a class with about a dozen men and two other women.

The surprising strategies that we were taught on how to navigate curves apply to our topic of goal-setting. You would think that the best way to navigate a curve on a motorcycle would be to follow the middle line as it curves with the road, concentrating on the five or ten feet in front of you. But that's not what we were taught. To smoothly ride through a curve, you focus on the end of the curve, not a short distance in front of you. Believe it or not, when you look ahead to your destination, you lean the motorcycle into the curve at just the right angle to get you there like a pro. You are looking ahead to where you want to end up. And that's also the best approach to setting goals.

Before we continue to talk about goals, I can't resist telling you about the challenging requirements of the course. On the second day, one of the women became discouraged and decided to drop out of the class. On the third day, another woman was pulled out of the line by the instructor while we were doing "figure-eights" on the motorcycles. She was told that she wasn't performing well enough to continue the course and was advised to start over on another date. Whoa! Can you imagine how I felt? I was now the only woman left in a class that included some big, burly Atlanta police officers. I was more determined than ever to finish the class, but I had to admit that it shook me up a bit.

At the end of the fourth day, when we took our riding test, I was really nervous. Frankly, the paper and pencil test had been easy for me. I'm good at academics. But the riding test was difficult, with all kinds of situations thrown at me where I had to make decisions in a split second. I knew that it was going to be difficult because we had practiced and practiced all of the maneuvers that would be included in the test, so I knew what was coming. Just before it was my turn to take the riding test, I walked over to some trees and sat down, took some deep breaths, and told myself, "You can do this. You have been doing this in the class. Now get out there and ride." I passed, even though I was wobbly once going through some cones.

I'm sharing my story because I know that my determination to achieve a goal applies to you. When you believe that you can accomplish a goal, then you tell yourself that you will make it happen, and you start taking the steps toward success. In my example, I signed up for a course, and participated in all the aspects of the course for four days until I was successful. Let me say that if I had let my motorcycle fall, which is an automatic fail, or just gotten too tired to finish the class, that would have been all right, too. I could have just signed up again like I hope those other two women did. It is important to keep going, to have perseverance. It could have taken me many times to pass. All I would have done is used up more of my time and money. But the key is to not give up.

Laughter is good for the soul, so here's the comedian W.C. Fields talking about setting goals:

> *"If at first you don't succeed, try again. Then quit. No use being a damned fool about it."*

Sometimes, just lightening up and not taking something so seriously can help relieve some pressure! Actually, being able to laugh at yourself is so helpful.

Some of the goals that you list may be very realistic, like being able to walk around the block. Most of you could accomplish that goal by walking a little more each day. Just be sure that you are specific about what distance you will add each day or week.

Then there are seemingly impossible goals. Personally, I like the thrill of taking on a big challenge. I guess there's a balance between what can realistically be achieved and a goal that is so far out there that it seems impossible. Here's another story, which may not be entirely accurate, to inspire you:

> *Colonel Sanders tried some ventures that were not successful and then he got the idea that he could make money from his mother's fried chicken recipe. He made*

some unsuccessful attempts to capitalize on her recipe before he had the idea to offer franchises. And the rest is history, as they say. His first ideas didn't get the desired result, but he was persistent.

Here are some of the points we have covered so far:

1. Focus on the biggest dream first, the dream that would make a difference in your life.
2. Research what steps you would have to take to reach that dream.
3. Be willing to be flexible. If your first idea doesn't work, go to Plans B or C.

So, you might start with a 5- year plan or you might start with a one-year plan. Then you can add monthly goals, weekly goals, and daily goals. I like lists so that I can check off what I've done. I like a planner. Mine is the old-fashioned paper version with dividers for months of the year and days of the week. Each day has an hourly schedule. I like to schedule when I'm going to do what. I fill in the goals in a section, "To be done today" with lines and little boxes to check off. You may not need to be so detailed. But it's motivating for me to check the boxes. You probably do your planning in a phone or computer. Whatever works to get you on track.

Make a timeline so you have a completion date in mind. Then schedule segments of time to devote to checking off the smaller goals. I accomplish much more when I structure my time. When I was in college, I liked to schedule time to study in the library between classes. When I went directly to the library after class, I wasn't tempted to go back to the dorm and study with all the distractions that come with dorm life. I was also using time efficiently. I thought, "While I am on campus, I'll just go ahead and get my research done." Telling you this reminds me of something else that was important to me. Physical space.

CREATE A SPACE
TO PLAN AND WORK

When I was in college, I noticed that I looked forward to research time if I liked the physical space where I studied. When I was a student at Pittsburg State University in Pittsburg, Kansas, I loved a particular place in the library. What we called the "stacks" was an upstairs area with translucent floor tiles that minimized the lighting to preserve the rare books. I thought that space was beautiful.

I guess that's analogous to you finding a place where you enjoy working. Or dreaming of having a beautiful space of your own someday. As we talked about before, place can be important. Some places are energizing for you and some places make you feel smothered or depressed.

Okay, let's get to your specific goals.

Five-year goal or One-year goals: If five years just seems too overwhelming, stick with just an annual goal. So, if you go with a one-year plan, then you can specify what you will get done each month, week, and day as the steps to reach your one-year goal.

For a five- year plan, list the goals that you plan to accomplish each year. A possible five- year plan would be saving a certain amount of money each year so that you can afford to buy land and build a house. Another example of a four or five-year goal would be completing an educational degree. Yet another example of annual goals that get you closer to a five-year completion date would be planting trees that take years to produce fruit or to be ready to sell as Christmas trees.

Whether you start with a five-year plan or a one-year plan, begin by stating what the long-range goal is. Then break it down into steps. So, for a goal that you estimate will take one year to complete, define that big goal. Then, develop monthly, weekly, and daily goals take get you closer to the big goal.

BE AS SPECIFIC AS POSSIBLE WHEN YOU LIST YOUR GOALS.

If your goal is to buy some land and build a house, where are you going to look for land and what will the blueprints for the house plan look like? If you are planning to get a college degree, what college will you attend and what will you study? If you are planning to start a business selling fruit trees, what kinds of fruit trees will you grow? How much time does it take for the trees to bear fruit? Do they have to cross-pollinate? What region of the country is best suited for certain trees? …Get the idea?

When you think of this exercise as objectively as possible, you realize that you are creating a life plan much as a company develops a business plan. Then you realize that you have a lot at stake here. You are going to set aside time, energy, and perhaps money to achieve your dream. It's important. You're important. Your life is important.

To achieve your individual goals, it is necessary to believe that it can really happen. Believing that the opportunities and resources will be there when you are ready requires a certain way of thinking. You no longer limit yourself with thoughts like "I'll never have enough money." Instead, you know that there is plenty. Plenty of ideas, plenty of resources, and plenty of choices.

Chapter 16

There's Plenty

Especially during difficult times, you may tend to put on blinders, so that you only see what is right in front of you. Sometimes I give the example of a little mouse who can't see beyond his whiskers. You might concentrate only on the source of your distress and constrict your thinking to what caused the problems and how much you are struggling.

This process narrows your vision so that you don't see all of the possible alternatives. Whether you are grappling with solving a specific problem or dealing with a particular situation, you might put up a shell and stay inside it. Inside your "cave," you can spend hours obsessing on negative outcomes and creating self-defeating thoughts.

When you narrow your vision, you can't see outside of your self-made wall. But suppose a helicopter swooped down and scooped you high up into the sky. Now you can see for miles in all directions, and the higher you go, the bigger area you can see. **When you transcend your limited view, your awareness broadens.**

When you go beyond your little world, your

perception of the range of options changes. Now you can see almost infinite possibilities for solving that problem, dealing with that situation, or setting limitless goals for yourself. You begin to **realize that "there's plenty."**

STRATEGIES FOR KNOWING THAT THERE'S PLENTY

When I reflect on how I have gotten through some tough times, I realize that one of the keys for me has been to send out grateful thoughts to God for the blessings that I have been given. Instead of dwelling on what I don't have, I focus on what I have. When you see life as a gift, you are grateful for everyone and everything that you have been given.

Reflecting on what you have been given calms you so that you can see that there's plenty more. There are plenty of ways to make a living. There are plenty of places to live. There are many people who can potentially be your companions.

The older I get, the more grateful I become. Gratitude for what you have sends out a message that you appreciate everything that makes your life more enjoyable and more meaningful. You are acknowledging that you know that there are many ways that the future can materialize.

Waking up in the mornings with a grateful attitude is so important. Be grateful for your life.

Be grateful for your health. Be grateful for the opportunity to enjoy another evening with a beautiful cloud formation or another night sky full of stars. I live simply, and maybe that increases how much I enjoy just being alive. I notice the simple things.

This morning, while I was drinking coffee on the porch, I was delighted to see the first bluebirds of the season making a nest in the birdhouse by the garden. And then as I checked the news on my phone, I read about an asteroid, or as the writer called it, a "mini-planet" that has whirled into the earth's gravitational pull and is circling the earth. The last time that a similar phenomenon was noticed by NASA was 2006, when an asteroid circled our planet for about a year before hurtling back out again. How interesting is that! And there are millions more asteroids and stars and planets and galaxies out there to ponder.

When I went out to weed the garden this week, I noticed that the gaillardia plants have sprouted back up after spending the long winter months under the ground. I was so happy to see them. And, the spectacular miracle was the butterfly chrysalis hanging on my garden fence. How I wish that I could witness the caterpillar's transformation into a winged butterfly.

There's a lot going on. You just have to take the time to notice. So, there's plenty of life happening.

There are plenty of stars and planets and asteroids. There are also plenty of ideas and plenty of opportunities.

One of the mistakes that I see people make that contributes to their unhappiness is thinking that when they lose a job, a significant relationship, or a house, that they will never have another. "I'll never get another job that good," is a sure way to forecast a future of gloom. If you **believe** that you just lost the best job that you will ever have, then you're right. It is so much better to believe that there are plenty of jobs. You may not get paid as much, but maybe you will enjoy the next job more. Or maybe the next job has more opportunities to climb the ladder.

The same erroneous thinking often happens with relationships. "If she leaves me, I'll never find someone else." Really? One of my silly responses to this irrational thinking is, "There are over seven billion people living on this planet. Approximately half are male and the other half are female. The odds of finding a new partner are actually pretty good." **Of course, to find another mate, it helps to be open to possibilities and not limit your choices**. What I want to do for you is to minimize the fear that you might experience in situations involving loss.

It doesn't help when music lyrics send out messages like "He's the only one for me" or "She's my reason for living." Ouch! Silly romantic ideas like these make it sound like there's only one person in the world who can add to your enjoyment of life. **Let me tell you a very exciting fact. There's plenty.**

WHEN YOU BELIEVE THERE'S PLENTY, THEN YOU OPEN UP TO MANY POSSIBILITIES.

When you're open to experiences and possibilities, a whole new world appears before your eyes. Now, you're noticing job listings and people and houses that were not in your awareness when you were in the "there's only one" thinking mode. You start expecting more possibilities.

On television, Netflix features some great shows on the many, many kinds of residences that people can build or renovate. People renovate old churches or railroad depots or even boats. They say that they love living a bit differently from the usual house or apartment. I know you've heard of "tiny homes." Well, some begin as storage bins or school buses. There are plenty of ideas for how to live. Then there are the really adventurous folks who live off the grid, with no running water or electricity in some remote woodland, and **they seem to have plenty to be happy about.**

Open yourself to the possibilities. Do some Google searches on types of houses. You will probably be amazed and inspired by how creative people can be in their choices of residences. For very little money, you can build a house out of recycled materials. You can live under the ground. You can live on the water. I'm going on and on here to make the point that there's plenty.

There are also plenty of ways to further your education or attain a new skill. There are plenty of ways to meet people, especially now with the help of meet ups and other social media inspired gatherings. There are plenty of ways to make money. Instead of working one 40-hour-a-week job, how about working two or three part time vocations. I have been a mental health counselor, a group facilitator, a college professor, a realtor, and a bookstore salesperson in all kinds of combinations.

I have noticed in my life that when I have the least, then a great idea often comes to me. For example, I was literally living in a tent when it occurred to me that this might be the time to get my Ph.D. The children were grown. It would be easy to move to wherever since I wasn't trapped by a house. I would qualify for a student loan since I was single and had little money. This was a dream I had carried with me for over 30 years. When I was about 26 years old, my boss at Parsons State Hospital and Training Center in Kansas said to me, "Laurie, you should get your Ph.D." The thought had not occurred to me. Psychologist Dan Smith gave me the idea.

Unfortunately, the timing wasn't right. So, years went by and circumstances changed, but Dan had planted a seed in my mind and heart. Then, 30 years later, in 2003, when I was 56 years old, and frankly very open to what might come next, that idea reappeared. It might have seemed like a stupid idea to many people. First, I was 56 years old. Second, I had very little money. The practical thing to do would be to take that full-time management job that I was offered at the local Home Depot. But, for me, making a dream come true was more rewarding.

I had dreamed of getting a Ph.D. for 30 years. I believed that I could make it come true. I have to admit that some schools were not interested in this enthusiastic woman who wanted to get a Ph.D. after being out of school for many years. I researched many schools, even one in San Francisco. I decided that San Francisco was not possible because the cost of living was so high. An administrator at Emory University suggested that I get another Master's degree, instead of a Ph.D. But the University of Georgia welcomed me with lots of interest in my professional experience and offered me an opportunity to be a doctoral student in their Educational Psychology department.

When it's time to reassess your life, don't search for security. **Frankly, security from things is just an illusion.** Job security is a myth because the company might go bankrupt or morph into an online version of itself. A relationship, not counting your relationship with God, of course, doesn't offer security because that person might leave you or die. And a certain house doesn't represent security because it, too, might be a thing of the past in a divorce or a bad storm.

Actually, on this earth, there is no such thing as security. Government jobs used to be thought of as offering "job security." That was not true. Or being able to stay with a corporation for 40 years until you retired. That's a fantasy, too. Stop looking to jobs, people, and houses as sources of security. Instead, ask yourself what you would enjoy, who you would enjoy spending time with, and where you would enjoy living. Security is a myth, and it is over-rated.

YOU ARE WISE WHEN YOU KNOW THAT THERE ARE INFINITE POSSIBILITIES.

You are connected to a big web of existence. You are not alone. Your mind cannot even imagine what's possible. That's how expansive reality can be. When you are grateful and you make the effort, your attitude and hard work will be reciprocated by a generous, plentiful circle of life. When you put ideas out there, they will be received, and more ideas will come to you.

The manifestations of your trust can come in

many forms. So, again, be open to possibilities. Know that there is plenty. Don't expect new possibilities to look like your pre-conceived, limited ways of thinking. Be open to all kinds of possibilities for your life.

Expectations can limit you. Your dream house may not be what you initially envisioned. You can have pre-conceived expectations of how your future lover will look, for example. Or what they will do for a living. Let go of that. Also, realize that opportunities for taking a different path career-wise may appear when you least expect it. So, avoid having rigid expectations for when people and career opportunities and housing ideas may appear.

You might meet someone fascinating at a bookstore or even the grocery story. A career idea may come seemingly out of nowhere while you are walking your dog. You may see an idea for a new residence in a movie you are watching just for entertainment. I swear that sometimes it seems to me that books almost literally fall off of bookstore shelves and into my hands because they want me to read them. I have gotten all kinds of inspiration from movies. And I do some of my best creative thinking when I'm walking down the street.

There are infinite possibilities for your life. Just be open to when and how they will appear. That's the fun of it.

Chapter 17

Don't Let Fear Limit You

Fear of failure. Fear of being alone. Fear of looking silly. Fear of what others might think. Fear of losing everything. Fear of taking risks. Fear of choosing a career that you don't enjoy. Fear of moving to a city that you later decide is not a good fit. Fear of success. Fear of intimacy. Fear of not having enough money. Fear of losing your health. Fear of not getting approval. Fear of not being accepted. Fear of rejection. Fear of change.

The number of fears is almost overwhelming. Then there are the "in-your-face" fears, like fear of snakes, fear of spiders, and fear of storms. And the fears that others use to control us, like "You can't make it without me."

FACE YOUR FEAR

Let's talk about some strategies that you can use to decrease the fear in your life. The first is to **face your fear.** Instead of avoiding situations that are frightening, turn around and stare right at your fear. Write down your fears in your journal. Then actually say out loud what makes you afraid. Guess what?! It's okay to be afraid!

Which one of your fears has caused you to put off taking action by procrastinating? Or what about your excuses for not facing your **fear of change**, like "I think I'll just keep this job because I know I'll have a steady paycheck." It is better to be honest with yourself. Is that steady paycheck worth a life of boredom? Is it worth dreading to go to work in the mornings? This is your valuable life that we are talking about. **Are you going to allow fear to limit your choices? The answer is "No."** When you realize that you can be afraid and still move forward, then you're not immobilized by your fear.

So, how do you move forward and feel fearful at the same time? First, specifically **define your fears.** What are the fears that are limiting your choices? What are the fears that are dictating how you feel about yourself? What are the fears that are trapping you in a boring job or a house that is too much to maintain?

You might say to yourself, "I am putting off starting my own business because I'm afraid I won't have enough income." When you write this down and really look at it, you realize that you are stalling for a rational reason. You do need a certain amount of money to have decent housing and food on the table.

Now that you have looked at the situation, you can let go of the confining "all-or-nothing"

thinking. You don't have to hurry and quit your job and plunge head-long into your new business. You can take time to do some planning. How about starting to save money for that cute little boutique that you've been dreaming about while you continue your full-time job? You could start with little steps. That's not so frightening.

If the thought of downsizing from the big house that you no longer need is overwhelming, why not share your trepidations with a trusted friend. You can even share with them what you're really feeling. You feel fear about leaving the home that you have lived in for 30 years. You could even add that you are afraid to move to a new residence in a new city. **When you share your burden, there's not so much for you to carry.**

How about asking friends to help you discard everything that you're not taking to your smaller abode? One step at a time. One room at a time. Now, your fear has been acknowledged, the undertaking seems more manageable when you have help, and your fear takes a back seat.

THE STRATEGY IS TO
ADMIT THAT YOU'RE AFRAID.

It's okay to be afraid. Sometimes your fear is telling you to slow down and think about the steps necessary to get where you want to go. Or your fear may be telling you that it would be better not to always act so strong. Maybe your fear is urging you to share your concerns, so that your army of angels is alerted to show up to help.

When I decided to move to Ellijay, Georgia, after a divorce, I had enough money to buy some land and have a small log cabin built, but that left me with a very small financial cushion. There were days when I worried about money. There were days when I was not happy with my job and couldn't wait to get my own counseling business going. Even though I had a lot to deal with, I pushed forward and did my usual stoic "I'm so strong" routine.

I learned a valuable lesson one day getting my hair cut and colored. Someone had given me a rec-ommendation for a hair stylist, Mark Queen. I really liked the way that Mark Queen styled my hair…and I really liked Mark Queen. I had been to his salon many times when, one day, Mark fin-ished with his other clients before me, which left just him and me in the salon. We got into one of our usual interesting conversations. Then, some-how, the topic turned to me. Mark said, "You know, Laurie, sometimes it would be nice to see your vulnerability." I may not have the quote ex-act, but it's close.

That is some of the best advice I've ever gotten. He went on to say that when I would come in the salon, I was like the life of the party with my interesting life experiences and positive attitude. He pointed out, however, that it would be okay to be more real sometimes. He knew that living alone, working a full-time job and also working part-time to build up a counseling business wasn't easy. When he made that candid remark, it was like I gave a giant sigh of relief. Wow, I didn't have to seem like I was fearless all the time. I didn't have to give the impression that I had everything all figured out.

When "the cat was out of the bag" and I felt comfortable sharing my reality with someone, guess what, the fear dissipated. Instead of pretending that I had no fear, I could be honest with myself. **I could say, "I'm scared but I'm going to "do it anyway."**

BE AUTHENTIC WITH YOURSELF AND OTHERS

What hit me on the head that day was the importance of being authentic. It was also a life lesson in connecting with others. You don't have to take on the world all by yourself. You are not a better person because you don't ask for help. The statement, "I don't need anybody" is not true. We all need support and encouragement. Actually, you are being true to your real self when you share your burdens with trusted friends.

Years ago, Iceland was one of the countries that

was at the top of "The World's Happiest Countries" list. Even though the country is dark much of the year, most of the people in Iceland shared on a questionnaire that they were happy. Researchers have found that one of the reasons that Icelanders were happy was that they knew that someone had their back. The government at the time provided a financial support net. So that if someone wanted to start their own business, for example, there was access to some money. Also, there wasn't a status hierarchy with jobs. If you were a nurse, you were regarded with as much esteem as the head of the country. In summary, the happiest people felt as if they were supported and important.

Some of the studies of longevity have concluded that a sense of community is important to how long you live. **When you feel that you are connected to a community or a family or a friend, you are not as controlled by fear.** When you know that someone realizes who you really are and what you're really going through, then you don't feel so afraid.

Those of you who feel as if you "don't fit in" have a difficult time enjoying life and facing each day with courage and joy. When you feel as if you are accepted for who you are, being different does not elicit fear. In fact, you can celebrate your uniqueness. It is okay to hear the beat of a different drummer. This is one of the messages that Lady Gaga stands for and it obviously resonates with many of us.

Facing fear requires courage. Showing your vulnerability, sharing your fears, and summoning support is not easy. And, for many of us, it does not come naturally.

Sometimes, you might feel fear because you are afraid that when you make a change in your life, you will regret it. "What if I don't like my new job?" you might ask yourself. At least, if you keep the same job, you tell yourself, you know what to expect. Well, here's some good news: **It's okay to change your mind.**

YOU CAN CHANGE YOUR MIND AND YOUR LIFE PATH

If you change some aspect of your life and you don't like it, you can change your mind. You can completely change your life path, if you choose. Yes, it might be inconvenient. You might lose some money, if you have already invested in a course of study and then change your mind. But it's better to lose some money than to resign yourself to a career path that is not enjoyable or fulfilling.

There is no reward in "sticking it out" in a job that you don't enjoy. There is no reason to stay with a college major that you discovered after a few classes is not even interesting. There is no automatic ticket to heaven because you stayed in an abusive relationship.

Let me give you a rather shocking example from

my counseling practice in Douglasville. I was working with a woman in her 50's who came to me for therapy because she realized that many fears were holding her back, including a fear of flying. The saddest part to me was that her life dream was to be an archeologist, excavating in Egypt. She could not realize her dream if she would not fly.

Because I wanted to understand the "Why?" of her fears, I delved into family patterns. She disclosed that her father was abusive to her mother and to her. When she was very young, her father hung her out of a second-story bedroom window upside-down by her ankles to scare her into obeying.

As we explored what her mother was like, she said, "My mother was a saint for staying with my father." **There it was.** She was stuck, like her mother had been stuck. She had committed to her fears for a long time, just as her mother had made a commitment to her husband. She believed, deep down, that she could not make a change. She admired her mother for staying in a marriage in which she was abused and at least one of her children was abused. Unfortunately, the message that it is virtuous to "stand by your man" is still heard in popular music.

Sometimes, even after a woman has been beaten numerous times by her husband, she still declares, "I love him so much" as if it is some kind of badge of honor. As if she is declaring, "Even though I am afraid that he is going to hurt me again, it is admirable of me to still love him." And stay with him, in harm's way. She is not listening to what her fear is telling her. Her fear is telling her to get away, to move on, to free herself.

Don't be afraid of what others think. When you change course, they may call you irresponsible or say that you never finish what you start. Actually, the flexibility and willingness to change course is necessary to be successful.

Right now, retail stores are having a tough time realizing a profit because of the competition of online stores. Most "brick and mortar" stores are being coerced into having an online component. Now, you can order groceries or clothing or books online and the products will be delivered to your door the next day. Retailers have changed how they do business to keep up with the demand of the customers, like you and me. Some of the stores that have resisted change have closed.

You may make a decision about what to do for a living, and then change your mind. You may sell your house and move to another city, and then change your mind. You may start a certain kind of business, and then change your mind.

Let go of the fear of change. Let go of the fear of failure. Actually, there's no such thing as failure. Okay, you made an attempt at a business that did not have enough demand to stay afloat or at the time you didn't have the resources necessary to keep it going. That's not a failure. That's taking a risk. That's living life to its fullest. If you have not made mistakes, you have not lived a very interesting life. If you have not had a job or a relationship or a residence that didn't work out, then you have not been experimenting with choices. We learn from these life experiences!

Chapter 18

Trust Your Intuition

Have you ever had a **"gut feeling"** that it would be a good idea to take a certain course of action? Have you ever had a **"hunch"** that something would happen? Have you ever thought about someone for the first time in years, and then the phone rings and, guess what, it is that same long-lost friend on the line?

Maybe you have sensed potential danger in a person or a place. Maybe you had a strong feeling that a person walking close to you in a parking lot may bring trouble. Maybe you sensed an ominous feeling in a certain space.

Or, your experience could have been that, even when all the facts told you that a business idea wouldn't work, you had this nagging urge to go forward with the idea anyway. **If you quickly decide to implement a new marketing approach, despite all the rational factors that tell you it will be a mistake, that could be you trusting your intuition.** You might tell your fellow marketers, "I know that all of my experience tells me that this approach is ridiculous, but I just have this gut feeling that it will catch on." You have a "hunch" and you decide to go with it.

It's hard to put your finger on exactly what intuition is, but what I know is that intuition is not common sense. Intuition is like insight, without using reason. You act spontaneously or have a feeling about someone without knowing why. You might feel uneasy about a situation when all the tangible indicators point to a positive resolution. It's like a "knowing."

If you trust your intuition and the result is what you wanted, others may question, "How did you know that?" All you can say is, "I don't know." For example, your boss asks you and your co-workers for your opinions about hiring someone. All the usual indicators, like education, work experience, even references, say loud and clear that she would be a good fit for the company. You are the only one who resists and says, "I just have a feeling that you will regret it if you hire her." You are standing out on a limb here, but you are going with your gut. If this is really your intuition at work, sure enough, something about this new employee turns out to be disappointing.

THE WAY TO KNOW
THAT IT IS YOUR INTUITION
IS IF YOUR FEELING HAS
NOTHING TO DO WITH YOUR EGO.

Intuitive feelings come from a higher place. It's like you have a "Spidey sense" that is part of something bigger than you are. In Spiderman's case, the feelings were often ominous suspicions, but they were seemingly irrational at the time, or rational, depending on the situation.

Do you remember James Redfield's books, *The Celestine Prophecy* (1993) and *The Tenth Insight* (1996) in which the main character goes off to another country to find a friend who is missing? All through his journey, he relies on "insights" to guide him to the next person who will help him find his friend or the next place that will get him closer to finding her.

He might be eating a bowl of soup and all of a sudden "know" that he needs to move on, even though the villagers are friendly and providing him with food. It was like "I've got to go right now" with no obvious reason. Or like "We need to go this way" when the main character really didn't know where he was going. This is a good example of trusting your intuition.

The word "intuition" may come from the Latin verb, "intueri" which means "consider" or it may come from a Middle English word, "intuit" which means "to contemplate." Maybe, somehow, you have had the experience that you have considered and contemplated, albeit quickly, and you have a comprehension of what is true. It does seem that your intuition often kicks in when you are in a quiet, receptive state of mind. You have an inner knowing.

I'm encouraging you to listen to yourself and trust your intuition. You won't be able to explain how you know, but that's okay. Consider your intuition to be a personal power. **Trusting your intuition increases your personal power.**

INTUITION CAN BE A POWERFUL GUIDE

Ask for signs to guide you. Expect the "messages" to come at any time, in any place. Intuition probably comes directly from your unconscious. Remember how I mentioned that your dreams are raw, uncensored data that can be valuable sources of information? Intuition is also uncensored data. Your ego has nothing to do with intuition. Your ego is located in your conscious self which deals with all of the extraneous happenings going on around you. Intuition comes from within the unconscious.

One of the reasons that it is tempting to ignore your gut feelings is that you can't point to anything outside of yourself for a rational explanation of how you know whatever it is. That goes counter to everything you are taught in school about having "evidence" for your conclusions. Here's the way I look at it. There are just things you can't explain but you know that they exist.

One of the signs that I experience frequently is synchronicity. Some days, I feel as if the stars are aligned in my life and I'm in sync with the universe.

I feel connected to some bigger force that is guiding me to who to connect with and where to go to make the connection. Sometimes, the same theme reoccurs all day long. When I trust my intuition, I see the signs and I see the patterns. Actually, I expect signs to come to me and messages to guide me. I don't really believe in coincidences, so I see meaning in my perceptions.

Your intuition is designed for the purpose of guiding you. Sometimes your intuition is protecting you from harm. Your intuition could be guiding you in the direction of a course of action regarding a problem that you have been wrestling with. Maybe you are introduced to someone and you have this overwhelming feeling that this person is not to be trusted. That is your intuition warning you to avoid a relationship with this person and, perhaps, to warn someone else not to pursue a relationship with him.

In 1992, *Women Who Run with the Wolves,* a fascinating book by Clarissa Estes hit the market. One of the wise lessons contained in the book was **the importance of trusting your gut.** When women "run with the wolves" they are aware of danger. Wolves seem to be wired to sense possible danger. Some women, those with a heightened awareness, sense danger and quickly avoid certain people or situations. One of the author's points was that many women have lost their ability to sense physical or emotional danger.

For example, two women may go to a party together. Each woman is asked to dance by the same man. They both accept. But one woman immediately senses that this guy is not to be trusted and is probably dangerous. The second woman dances with the same man, but has a totally different perception. She falls head over heels in love and gets in a serious relationship with him. The man turns out to be controlling and abusive. The second woman later confesses that she made a huge error in judgment.

The first woman paid attention to her intuition. The second woman was distracted by exterior superficial factors, like how good-looking and charming he was. It would have been better if the second woman had paid attention to the signs of danger. She paid a price for not paying attention to her gut.

Sometimes your body tells you that you are choosing to ignore signs of either pending danger or pending success. I got the hives years ago when my body was telling me that I was pursuing a relationship that was not in my best interest. My body was alerting me to the possible negative consequences. Another way that I respond to stress, in addition to feeling really anxious, is what doctors call "frequency of urination." I have to go to the bathroom every five minutes, which is really annoying when I'm sleeping. Sometimes, before I can put words to what I am experiencing, my body will tell me. Pay attention to signs from your body.

INTUITION IS
LIKE A SUPER POWER

Intuitive ability is very powerful. To be happy, it is important to feel personally powerful. Trusting your intuition is a choice, perhaps made on an unconscious level, that increases your power. You can be discerning about what others' motives really are or what actions someone is going to take, regardless of what they say. Or, if you don't trust your intuition, you can choose to ignore your gut feelings. You can sometimes predict outcomes, even if your "information" is not as specific as you would like.

I think that intuition is a deeply ingrained survival tool that many of us have forgotten is important. We have gotten out of practice in the use of this tool. We make the mistake of not paying attention to our intuition because we think we are silly for believing something intangible, not provable, not measurable, not scientific, not rational, and not reasonable. When we limit ourselves to only believing what we can actually see with our eyes or hear with our ears, we miss the non-tangible message that is urging us to take action.

I encourage you to learn to trust your intuition. Don't get talked into anything that doesn't "feel right." Learn to be very proactive and deliberate about the people that you allow into your energy sphere. You do not have to be nice to everyone. Trust your gut and courageously walk away if you sense danger. When you trust your intuition, you trust yourself. You are building your self-confidence.

Listening to your intuition is a skill that you can develop. Take time to listen. Take the time to be still with a thought. Ask for guidance. Pay attention to subtle messages and trust your gut when you are making decisions.

The other night I was watching "Shark Tank," a television program in which people pitch their business ideas to a panel of successful investors. On this particular show, one of the men who approached the millionaires with his idea was indecisive about which offer to accept. **I was pleasantly surprised to hear the advice of one of the potential investors. He asked, "What does your gut tell you?"**

Here was a successful businessman who is usually crunching numbers to decide whether to invest in a particular business idea. And yet he was advising someone just entering the business market to trust their intuition. It isn't always the most seemingly reasonable approach which is the best fit for you.

Increase your awareness to include what you can't explain. Don't discard your hunches and gut feelings just because they are not measurable or because you can't prove how they work. When you have a strong hunch, pay attention to it. Don't discard it as being silly. Really consider your gut feelings and hunches.

Intuition is the voice of your soul speaking. I suggest that you keep a record in your journal of times during the day that you had a hunch or a gut feeling. Intuition is like a "knowing voice" that senses the directions that would be most beneficial to you as you move forward with your life. Record how you responded to the hunch and whether that led you to useful information.

A meaningful life is showcased by intuition, being able to "see" what is really going on around you and being able to forecast what might happen if you took a certain path. I believe that we have all been outfitted with intuitive ability, but that some of us have forgotten what a valuable tool intuition can be. As we forgot about this gift, we also discounted this important ability.

Trust yourself and pay keen attention to your intuition.

Chapter 19

What Gives
Your Life Meaning?

What gives your life meaning is a sense of purpose. When you know your purpose, then you can clarify the direction that you are going with your life. Take the time to articulate how your life adds to the greater good. I know that you and I are here on this planet for a reason. You were given certain talents and passions. You choose what you want to accomplish with them.

It takes a lot of **reflection and soul-searching** to decide what you want to achieve. To get you focused, it's helpful to write down where you see your journey going. This leads into some pretty deep questions, like "What is my reason for being?" and "Who do I want to impact?"

No matter what your age or where you are in your life, taking the time to chart a life course is a meaningful venture. Don't get too uptight about it, though. **You can always change your mind.** So, just start by asking yourself some questions:

1. What does your life look like today? Now, imagine what you would like it to look like.
2. What would you like to achieve? What are you aiming for?

3. What do you value? What is important to you?
4. What are you doing when you feel as if you are using your time wisely?

I'll get you started by sharing my goal for this book:

> *My goal is to instill in others the belief that they can achieve whatever they set their minds on and meet any challenges with resilience when they know that they have choices in how they think, feel, and act.*

WHERE DO YOU START?

I realize that projecting your intentions for your life is a really difficult task. It might make it easier if we do a process of elimination. **You could start with what you don't want to do:**

1. What is **not** stimulating or exciting to you?
2. **What makes you feel drained or tired** just thinking of spending time doing it?
3. What do you think of when you think of **what you "should" do?**
4. **What makes the time just drag?**

Here's a personal example. Years ago, I had a summer job working for the Texas Employment Commission. A company listed a three-day job crunching numbers concerning accounts receivable and accounts payable for their business. My boss asked me if I would like to fill the position since it paid well and then, after three days, I could return to the job at the employment commission. I eagerly said "Yes." After the first day, I wished I had said, "No, thanks" because the work was so boring and tedious to me. At that point in my life, I said, "That was the longest three days of my life. Thank goodness it was only for three days." I learned quickly that any position that included accounting is not how I want to spend my time. Even though I am good in math, I don't enjoy that kind of work and I certainly don't find it meaningful. But some people, like income tax accountants, for example, enjoy helping people by analyzing all of the factors pertaining to their taxes.

Hopefully, this helps you think of similar experiences that you have had. An approach for students would be to think of subjects that you don't like in school. Apparently, you don't find that spending time on those topics to be a meaningful use of your time and energy.

Now, on the flip side, here are some questions that might tip you off to **what you do find interesting and meaningful:**

1. **What puts you in "flow" where time seems to fly by?** You look up to check the time and find that three hours have passed when you would have sworn it was only an hour.

2. What would you enjoy doing, knowing that the results are meaningful?

3. What would **stretch you out of your comfort zone**? A meaningful use of your time comes with challenges that encourage you to grow.

4. What would make you **proud of yourself**? You would feel proud to be a part of a certain mission or, when you have accomplished what you set out to do, you want to share your achievements with others.

Once you discover what adds meaning to your life and then pursue that path, you will begin to create happiness. When you get clear on accomplishing something that makes sense to you, that energizes you, that causes you to get up every morning looking forward to an interesting day, then you will have arrived at your purpose.

BELIEFS THAT MAKE YOUR LIFE MEANINGFUL

There are many beliefs that are shared by those of us who know that our lives have meaning because we are an integral part of a much bigger web of existence. Here are a few of those beliefs:

1. **Believing that you are a vital part of a bigger force adds to the meaning in your life.** It doesn't matter what you call the greater power that started and maintains

life. What does matter is that you know, without reservation, that you were created, along with all life forms, to continue and add to the evolution of the cycle of life.

2. **The belief that you are connected to every living thing.** There is a big web of existence and you are a key piece in the life process. I love how some Native Americans honor the life force in all things. For example, they refer to trees as the Standing People and rocks as the Stone People. By acknowledging the life force in trees and rocks and the sun and the moon, they acknowledge that everything emits energy and everything has a purpose. It is important to realize that all of these life forms can help each other and help human beings.

3. **The belief that we play an essential role in the whole of creation.** The whole of creation is so intricately designed that our minds cannot comprehend the enormity of the process. The intelligence and creativity of the evolving life process deserves our awe and wonder. What we know, as so many wise people have said before me, is that we are all related.

4. **The fourth essential belief is that you can share energy with every living thing and every living entity can share energy with you.** It has been proven that when you talk to plants, they grow faster. Ok, ok, you

might think I've gone a little too far here. But I am serious when I tell you that the conclusions of scientific studies are that plants respond to the human voice.

In the studies, there were two sets of plants that were grown from seeds that were started on the same dates. There are various studies, so let's say that at the beginning of the study the plants each have four or five leaves. Both sets of plants get the same care. They have the same type of soil. They are given the same amount of water each day. They have the same amount of sunlight. The variable is that one set of plants in cared for in silence, while someone talks to the other set of plants each day. You guessed it. The second set of plants that heard the human voice daily grew at a faster rate. The plants were stimulated by the human voice and responded by growing faster.

Now, you might be wondering how other living entities can communicate with you. One example is the stones that I mentioned previously. Some rocks and stones give off vibrations that energize us humans. I told you that I have a stone that I keep close by for writing. I also have a piece of quartz I clutched in my palm during a tragic time to give me strength.

Another example of how trees and other leafy plants share energy with humans is that they give off oxygen that is essential for human life. I walk frequently at our local shopping mall. One reason that I feel invigorated in that environment is that there are dozens of live trees and shrubs giving off oxygen. Also, in my garden to each side of a two-person bench are lots of banana trees growing. They provide shade, so that I can sit comfortably and contemplate between weeding or harvesting sessions. They also share their energy with me.

This reminds me of a time years ago when I was very troubled about a relationship. I had read a few pages of Hugh Prather's inspirational book, *Notes to Myself*, and decided to take my thoughts outside to the night sky. The sky that night was full of bright stars, and as I searched for answers, I was comforted by their presence. I walked for a long time, just the stars and me, until I felt some peace of mind. I knew without a doubt that I was not alone in my struggles. I was part of this vast universe that welcomed me and accompanied me in my distress.

Another time when I was wrestling with a difficult decision, Mother Earth helped me. I had driven to Savannah, Georgia, to attend a conference of the Licensed Professional Counselors Association. Although I had the opportunity to stay in the hotel where the conference was headquartered, I chose to sleep in my tent in a little mom and pop campground outside of town. As I explained to one of my friends, I wanted to sleep in my tent close to the ground so I could feel the heartbeat of the earth. That experience provided the sense of connection that I needed. God even threw in an opportunity to have a meaningful conversation with a couple of campers in the next tent site.

That connection with all living things has been real to me since I was a child, and for that I am grateful. I hope that you spend time in nature and develop the belief that you, too, are connected to the universal web of existence. **Your life has meaning because you have an essential relationship with all other living things.** How will you choose to use your unique talents and gifts to further the evolvement of the creative life cycle and add further meaning to your life?

Chapter 20

Flexibility
Expands Your Mind

You're not going to be surprised to hear me say that you have a lot of **choices** concerning the ways you use your gifts and talents. I want to expand on that thought by encouraging you to not get too attached to any particular choice. There is not just one way to use your talents. There are many. If your first choice doesn't work out, be flexible and go with another option.

Consider the following possibilities regarding **the advantages of being flexible**:

1. Sometimes situations change or one option is no longer available.
2. Your idea of what's best for you may not really be what's best for you. Maybe God has another idea.
3. You make decisions based on the information that you have, which is usually incomplete.
4. You might work with one choice for a while, which will lead you to another opportunity and yet another opportunity.

Let me give you an example of number one on my list, that sometimes situations change or one option is no longer available. Suppose you have applied to a number of colleges. Even though you applied to many different colleges to increase the probability of being accepted into at least one, you really have your heart set on one particular college. You have done some research on the programs that interest you and the faculty in those departments. You even visited the campuses of three of your choices. One seemed a better fit. You really liked the faculty and the students that you met and the campus was beautiful.

The letters start to arrive from the colleges, informing you of whether or not you were accepted. Let's say that you were accepted to three out of the five that you applied to, but the college that was your number one choice did not accept you. You are disappointed. Your disappointment is natural. But, after reality sinks in, then it's important to move forward and make another choice from the colleges that accepted you.

BEING FLEXIBLE IS AN IMPORTANT INDICATOR OF YOUR RESILIENCE

Resilience is your ability to accept situations, bounce back, and navigate through whatever is put in front of you. Look at what the opposite of being flexible would look like. What if you are so heartbroken over the rejection by the college that was your first choice that you wouldn't consider going to any of the other colleges? You are so rigid, so narrowly focused on just one choice that you refuse to consider your other options. **Having flexibility means that you will consider many choices. When you are flexible, you are able to expand your mind to see that there are other ways to get where you want to go and to consider the possibility that you might actually be just as happy with another choice**.

I guess the term commonly used for being flexible is "going with the flow." Another saying I've heard is to "take it in stride." Some of the studies I mentioned in a previous chapter included interviews with centenarians, people who have lived to be over 100 years old. "What is your secret to living so long?" they were asked. One of the answers was that they "took things in stride" and didn't allow their distress over a situation to immobilize them.

Having several possible plans in mind creates the flexibility to go from one to another. You can say to yourself, "If Plan A doesn't work out, then I'll go to Plan B, and if that doesn't work out, I'll go to Plan C." Let's say that you are planning on remodeling your house. You had certain ideas about changes that you wanted to make, including new appliances and lighting fixtures and furniture. When you look up the prices of your Plan A, you realize that the cost is far more than you had budgeted to spend. So, you go to Plan B, where you cut costs by buying used furniture or less expensive lighting. Or you might complete part of the work now and then save to complete the rest of the work later. Plan C might be to toss the idea of renovation altogether and instead invest that chunk of change in a different house. That reminds me of a television show in which couples are indecisive about whether to renovate or to sell and they consider the arguments of both scenarios.

YOUR IDEA OF WHAT'S BEST FOR YOU MAY NOT BE WHAT'S BEST FOR YOU

At some point in your life, you may think you know what's best for you when it is not what's best for you. Relationships are easy examples of this point. You may have been in a relationship for a long time, and you have told yourself that this woman is the one for you. But when it gets more serious and you're contemplating a commitment, then you might start to really delve into all the dynamics of a marriage. After some serious discussions with your lover, you may be shocked to realize that the two of you do not have common goals.

For example, let's say that the person that you thought you were going to spend the rest of your life with now tells you that they don't want to have children. Whoa! You had just assumed that everyone who gets married wants to have children, but that is obviously not true. You are adamant about having children. That has been a life goal for years, and you are not going to change course on that part of your life.

Now the person that you thought was the best choice for a life partner is no longer the best choice for you. One of the purposes of a relationship is to be able to accomplish more together then you could individually. If you are not going to compromise your plan to have children, then it would be better to be flexible and start looking for someone who shares your dreams. If you rigidly stay in this relationship and "sell out," you will be miserable. Or it could go the other way. The other person wants to have children and you don't. Either way, what's best for you is to choose another life partner who has the same vision for a relationship. In this case, being flexible looks like letting go of one choice and making another choice.

Sometimes, what you thought was best for you was not a reflection of the highest idea of yourself. God may intervene and signal you to make another choice. I adore the television show, "God Friended Me" that is on Sunday nights. The premise of the program is that God, or someone pretending to be God, has friended a young man named Miles, who does not believe in God. To make it more interesting, Miles' dad is a bishop in a church. Anyway, Miles broadcasts a podcast where he expounds on his ideas about life.

Since Miles does not believe in God, he believes that a person pretending to be God is sending him "friends" via social media. Because Miles is curious, he follows up on the friends' requests, and soon discovers that each friend that God suggests actually needs his help. He shares his dilemma with his friends and soon they start working together to help every person who is "sent by God."

Whether the friend requests are coming from God or an impersonator, they are drawing Miles to a higher calling than just sharing ideas in a podcast. Now he is out there helping people who really needed his help. I don't know if it is the screenwriters' intention, but my theory is that this is really God reaching out to Miles, encouraging him to use his compassion and talents to help those in need. He is now living his true purpose, and the highest idea of himself.

YOU MADE DECISIONS BASED ON WHAT YOU KNEW AT THE TIME

There are many examples of how you may have made decisions based on incomplete information and then changed your mind. One example is a job offer that you accepted, only to regret it later. When you started to work for this company, you didn't know that the company's profit was often at the expense of the consumer. The company produces products that are not healthy and may even be detrimental to the health of its customers and that conflicts with your value of integrity.

Or, after working at the company for a while, you realize that you just don't fit in with the personalities of some of the other employees. Maybe there's some back-biting or there's a lot of drama. Maybe some of the employees do just enough work to get by while you are expected to "pull up the slack." Sometimes, the "pros" of the job, like the salary, can outweigh the "cons' like the human dynamics. And sometimes, the situation is so dismal that you start looking for another job.

Another example of the need for flexibility is a situation in which a person misleads you. You were led to believe that he had a certain employment history, and then you learned that he lied. Or you learn that a person that you had been spending time with has a criminal past. This actually happened to me once. I was living in an apartment complex and made friends with some of my neighbors. We got together at my apartment for New Year's and we all contributed to the usual New Year's meal of navy beans, greens, and cornbread and had a good time. One of the neighbors actually recommended another one of the neighbors for a job. Then we learned that he was wanted by the police in another state. He was actually on the run. It was quite a shock.

The police made the decision for us about

whether or not to continue that relationship when he was hauled off in a patrol car. Plus, this was not an intimate relationship. Sometimes learning of a dark past or even just that somebody has lied about important details can put you in an awkward situation. That's when the flexibility to consider options for how to handle the situation is so helpful.

ONE CHOICE MAY LEAD TO ANOTHER OPPORTUNITY AND THEN ANOTHER OPPORTUNITY

In this case, you may have made a choice of a job and then get news of another job that pays more money and offers more possibilities for advancement. Let's say you like your job and you like the other people at the company. But the news of an opening with another employer has you curious and, frankly, interested. Although you had not thought about changing jobs for a while, this opportunity may be worth pursuing.

When you are flexible, you probably follow up and ask some questions to get more information. Then, if you are still interested, you arrange a meeting or you are invited to an interview. If you are not flexible, you don't follow up on another opportunity. You tell yourself that you haven't been with the company long, and you should be more loyal. Afterall, they have treated you with respect and the work has been interesting. I know that there are more variables here to consider, but my point is that flexibility allows you to consider options.

When you are flexible, you can entertain the idea of making a change. You are able to think differently. Your flexibility allows you to go from one plan to another. When one possible solution to a problem doesn't work, you can quickly go to an alternative solution. You can enjoy your life more when you don't get stuck with "Now what do I do?" Instead, you almost welcome the opportunity to change course. Even when times are tough, your ability to be flexible gets you through the hard place.

As I write today, on March 29, 2020, the world is in the midst of a coronavirus pandemic. The daily routines of most people have been interrupted with local, state, and federal requests to stay home and to "socially distance" at least six feet from each other to stop the spread of the virus. Many people cannot work at their office and are working from home. Some have lost their jobs in restaurants and bars, because those places have been closed except for drive-through, pick-up, or home delivery. The schools are closed for at least another month.

Now, this is a time when those who are flexible are going to manage by changing how they spend their time and perhaps changing where they work. School children are doing their schoolwork online instead of in a classroom. Makeshift hospitals are being created out of previously obsolete buildings, ships, and canvas tarps. Scientists are considering using a malaria medicine and other treatments to treat the coronavirus.

This is a situation in which the unexpected happened and people are being encouraged to be patient and calm...and flexible. Some people are spending their spare time delivering meals to the elderly. Cosmetics companies are making hand sanitizers. The pillow manufacturing company, My Pillow, is making face masks. Ford, General Motors, and Tesla are going to make ventilators. A cabinet company is also making desks for school children who are working on computers at home. Volunteers are making face masks out of cloth scraps that they had at home. A woman who has saved thousands of dollars "extreme couponing" for years is packaging boxes of necessities and delivering them to those in need.

The willingness to be flexible by re-purposing assembly lines, creating temporary hospitals, and bringing food to those who have lost their jobs is going a long way in helping each other in a crisis. Weather forecasters are even turning their living rooms or basements into temporary television studios where they now broadcast their forecast predictions. These examples certainly illustrate that there are many ways to get things done. There are many ways to help each other. There are many ways…and places…to work.

When a need arises, whether you are the one who needs help or you see an opportunity to help someone else, flexibility will serve you well in getting available resources for yourself or others. Helping other people is a meaningful way to be happy. Thinking of those who are desperate and coming to their rescue fills up your soul. Sometimes it is inconvenient to be flexible. It would be easier just to keep doing what you are doing the way you were doing it. And it's not usually a crisis like the coronavirus pandemic that calls us to be flexible, whether it's to lend a helping hand or figure out how to feed your family when the business that your family has run for three generations is forced to close its doors.

Have you seen the television program, MacGyver? The main character's ability to think of different ways to get his crew out of possibly life-threating dilemmas or to create makeshift tools out of what's at hand is the crux of the show. When the door that they could usually run through to safety is jammed or the airplane is going to crash, MacGyver saves the day with his knack for thinking flexibly. While some of the other characters are giving up and resigning themselves to not getting out of the latest fix alive, MacGyver thinks of a way.

Of course, MacGyver is a fiction show. But in your very real life, that ability to think of various solutions and endless possibilities will serve you well. Being able to bend with whatever life presents will keep you from breaking. And, when the situation isn't dire, being flexible can add a lot of fun to your life by allowing you to consider new ideas for your life.

Chapter 21

Use Your Imagination

When I have asked people why they think they are unhappy, they have often replied "I just feel stuck. Sort of like I'm trapped in a life that I don't enjoy, and I can't find a way out." Often, unhappiness just creeps up on you. Then you notice that you are feeling fatigued for no physical reason. Activities that would have been interesting to you in the past no longer seem interesting. I've even heard the reply, "Same crap, another day," which sounded so negative that my body had a painful visceral response.

It is clear to me that if someone describes their life in that negative way, that they are unhappy because **they can't imagine what it would be like to be happy**. When you are in a rut, tell yourself to open up your imagination. Focus your attention on formulating new ideas for your life. Imagine what a happy life would look like.

Brainstorming new ideas can be really difficult if you have been in the doldrums for a long time. You might have gradually gone more and more into a sort of cave where you have insulated yourself from the outside world. You may have dwelled on your problems so long that you cannot even imagine that there are solutions. I am here to tell you that you can imagine your life differently. **You can imagine ways to enjoy your life and to flourish, not just survive.**

HOW DO YOU GET YOUR JUICES FLOWING AND GET YOUR IMAGINATION WORKING?

This is the time to reach out to others. Enlist the help of friends, neighbors, or family to create new ideas for your life. In the business world, brainstorming is an everyday team strategy for creating ideas. For example, McDonald's has Hamburger University in Chicago, which is a training facility for those in management positions. I worked with a man years ago who had previously been in McDonald's management and had attended Hamburger University. From his viewpoint, it was a hotbed of ideas on managing and problem solving in a fast food setting.

One of the strategies that many businesses use to get ideas flowing for new products or new marketing methods is to gather around a table or a teleconference platform and just **brainstorm ideas.** They are told not to judge them or even critique them at first. Just say what comes into their mind. The intention is to get as many fresh ideas out there as the team can imagine. It doesn't matter if the idea seems impossible or far-fetched or costly. Each person's ideas add to the energy of the group, and before you know it, there may be 20, 30, or 40 ideas listed. When you are in an environment like this, where "anything goes," the ideas will flow out like water.

Successful businesses constantly incorporate new ideas to keep customers buying. The employees making the products or providing services and the people who are marketing the products and services want to feel that they can offer ideas without being knocked down or criticized. The CEO's of successful companies know that the more ideas that are generated, the higher the probability that a few really lucrative ideas will materialize.

You can use this same brainstorming strategy to generate new ideas for your life. Ask a few people for ideas about how to go forward with your life. Just say, "I'm feeling kind of stuck right now. I want to make some changes in my life. Do you have any ideas?" You may word it differently so that it sounds more like you would say it, but you get the general idea.

One of my life lessons has been to learn to ask for help and not play the "strong one," as I mentioned in a previous chapter. You may have the same tendency to think that you are supposed to figure it all out yourself. Maybe you even think that it is a sign of weakness to ask for help. Let me stop you there. We all need each other. Most of the time, we are better together than we are apart. Remember the old adage, "Two heads are better than one." That is definitely true most of the time.

Have you ever wrestled with how to arrange photographs on a wall? Or what color to paint the living room? When you asked a family member or a professional interior decorator for their opinions, it opened you up to new ideas. After hearing the thoughts of someone other than yourself, you might have said out loud, "I hadn't thought of that." That's why you may have hired the interior decorator, who studied the photographs and the wall, and immediately encouraged you to make a big display on one wall for impact. Oh, yes, and she also told you the latest trendy paint that would look great on your living room walls.

THE POWER OF IMAGINATION INCREASES WHEN THERE ARE MANY IDEAS TO CONSIDER.

You could not possibly know all the ways to solve a problem or just spruce up your life all by yourself. If your wallet is stretched to the max, and you need to cut expenses, maybe a friend has some ideas about cheaper places to live. You cannot know of all the places that you might move that would be cheaper. A friend might have just driven by a "For Sale" sign that you didn't see.

So, today you might approach a friend or family member or even a professional with, "I've been thinking of making some changes in my life. I think I need to shake things up a little to get myself energized. What do you think?" Whatever your problem or situation is, who in your life might have some ideas? What open-minded people do you know who likes to play with ideas?

When I had my therapy practice, I had to participate in a certain number of "continuing education credits" per year to maintain my license. The courses might vary from year to year, but the one course that we had to take every year was "ethics." One of the main reasons for the importance of knowing the latest laws was so you didn't get sued. But, one of the ethical tactics that was helpful to me was **"Consult. Consult. Consult."** In other words, you are less likely to make a mistake in judgment if you have consulted with at least one other professional about a situation. That's true, but I also got a lot of ideas that had nothing to do with ethics by consulting with colleagues.

I remember one time I was reflecting on the possible meaning of a client's dreams. I decided to bounce it off a colleague and see what their impression was. Immediately, he responded with his perspective on the meaning of the dream and his idea on how I could use that information to be helpful to the client. His thoughts gave me another perspective to consider.

This is really analogous to your life, too. You might just need a "sounding board." You might benefit from merely bouncing your ideas off an open-minded listener. Sometimes people might ask, "Do you really want to know what I think?" Your choice is to either answer, "Yes," or you can say, "I really just need you to listen, so I can sort out my thoughts."

EXPAND YOUR MIND BY EXPOSING YOURSELF TO NEW IDEAS.

Learn new ways to look at specific areas of interest. Expose yourself to people who push the limits. Tune into creative ways of thinking every day. **When you study successful people, like Bill Gates, Warren Buffett, and Elon Musk, you quickly find out that many are avid readers.** In fact, most successful people devote time each day to learning something new. Many schedule one to three hours a day to reading books, magazines, newspapers, and professional journals.

Set aside time each day to fill yourself with new information. When you add to your knowledge base, you open your mind and your imagination takes over. Use your imagination to open your mind to new ideas. Be open to different ways to think, to live, to work, to have fun, to relate to others.

Visualization is a helpful tool in making your dreams come true. You can make a collage of actual photographs or pictures from magazines. Picture yourself in the land of your imagination. See yourself with a brighter future. See yourself connecting with people that you can trust. See yourself enjoying life. What does that look like?

One of the reasons that I love to read is that when I visualize the scenes as I read, it's like I am really there alongside the characters. Last year, I read all of the *Game of Thrones* books that George R. R. Martin had written up to that point. As I read, I experienced almost literally being in the scenes. I was there listening to the characters interact with each other. I was there running with them to escape danger. I was there when they entered a pub and I immediately smelled the delicious aromas of onion soup simmering as the author described.

A vivid imagination adds so much richness and enjoyment to your life. Here are some questions to help you imagine your future life.

1. **What** does your happy future life look like?
2. **Who** are the people who are there? Are some of them in your life now and are some of them sort of facsimiles of the kinds of people that you would like to know?
3. If you imagined some people **who** you don't know now, what would they be like? What attributes of your future friends or colleagues would add enjoyment to your life?

4. **Where** do you see yourself living? Do you have a photo similar to your dream place?
5. **What** do you see yourself doing that is enjoyable?
6. **What** do you see yourself doing that adds meaning to your life?

Imagine a scene that includes the people that you enjoy being around or that add meaning to your life. Use your five senses to imagine the backdrop, the place where you want to be. And visualize what you are doing. This exercise makes your dreams seem more real.

Using your imagination is an example of expanding your mind. You see yourself creating possibilities for your own happiness and, perhaps, for the happiness of others. I want to note here that when you use your imagination, it takes you out of yourself and your own needs for a while. Sometimes imagining yourself helping someone else leads you to actually take action. And helping others is usually a "feel good" activity.

Use your imagination to create the life that you want. Here's a great quote:

> *"Rich people believe, 'I create my life.' Poor people believe, 'Life happens to me.'"*

> —T. Harv Eker,
> *Secrets of the Millionaire Mind*, 2005

The author's wise quote combines several of the

points that we have covered in this book, like taking control of your life. Of course, the book, *Secrets of the Millionaire Mind*, pertains to the attainment of money. However, you can be rich in many ways. Whatever your idea of success is, you can create it.

In another chapter, I mentioned the book, *Sapiens* (2015), by Yuval Noah Harari. A premise in his book was that the sapiens who used their imaginations survived and those who kept doing the same old thing did not survive. According to the author, about 2.5 million years ago there were many tribes of Sapiens, including Neanderthals. One reason that Neanderthals did not survive was that they kept making the same tools out of rock over and over instead of considering other ideas for getting work done. The key to the survival of some sapiens was that they traveled to different places, studied plant seasons and animal migrations. They were also innovative and experimented with new tools. They exposed themselves to new experiences and new ideas.

You can use your imagination to create new ideas for problem solving, as our ancestors did. **You can also use your imagination to move forward to a happier, more productive life.**

Chapter 22

Expanding or Limiting?

As you use your imagination to generate ideas, be aware that you may currently be carrying around some limiting ideas. **Some ideas expand your thinking and some ideas limit your thinking and limit your choices.** We are exposed to messages from our culture that condition us to have certain expectations.

Often, we are expected to have an "either-or" way of thinking about characters in movies. They are either good or bad, trustworthy or not trustworthy, generous or selfish. This overly simplistic approach to depicting characters in movies or television programs doesn't leave room for us to ponder possibilities. Could the character be a genius at solving crimes, and also have personal flaws that affect his life? An example is Tom Selleck's brilliant depiction of Jesse Stone in the series. Without seeming to be working hard to figure out who committed the crime, he thinks and thinks about possibilities, like who murdered the victim, for example, and why. He follows the clues until he solves the crime. In his personal life, though, the character, Jesse Stone, is still emotionally entangled with his ex-wife and he drinks too much alcohol at times. He is a complex character.

In other movies and television shows, the complexities of people are addressed and the fun of the story is figuring out "who done it." In the television program, "Manifest," part of the fascination for those of us who are avid watchers is the puzzling question of who to trust and who not to trust. Any preconceived ideas about who will live and who will die or who might want to harm you and who wants to help you are often dashed in a single episode.

Now, let's move from entertainment to the real world. **You may have some preconceived ideas about how you will know the truth. You may also have some preconceived ideas that limit your ability to see divine intervention.** Most of you probably are familiar with the story about the man who has climbed to the roof of his house in a flood and is pleading with God to help him. If you look online, you will see that there are many versions of the story, but they all have the same basic premise that goes like this:

> *A man has climbed up to his roof because of a flood. He pleads with God for help. Then some men in a rowboat paddle over close to his roof and offer to help. "Come on," they say. "Get in the boat before the water gets higher." The man replies that he has prayed*

> to God for help, thank you very much, and
> he stays on the roof. Then two men in a
> motorboat come by and offer to help the
> man get off the roof and into the boat. The
> man again replies that he is waiting for God
> to rescue him and declines their help. Next,
> a helicopter flies over and the passengers
> drop a rope down to bring the man to
> safety. He again will not accept the help
> because he says that God will show up
> shortly. After he drowns and goes to
> Heaven, he asks God why he didn't save
> him. God replies, "I did offer to help you. I
> sent you a rowboat, a motorboat, and a
> helicopter."

I love this story and I have repeated it many times to many people. **When you have an erroneous preconceived idea about how God works or who can be helpful or what would be an acceptable response or what a person with moral character looks like, you may make a mistake in judgment.** Or your preconceived idea may be that there is only one "soulmate" for you in the whole world or that only a certain person can help you in a particular situation. Or your preconceived idea about social class may restrict your idea of who is happy and who is not happy.

YOUR PRECONCEIVED
IDEAS MAY LIMIT YOUR CHOICES.

If you have preconceived ideas about how your future significant other will look or what she will do for a living, you may not recognize the potential in someone to be a really special life partner. If you have preconceived ideas about what your future home will look like or where it will be located, you may miss some great places to live. If you have already made up your mind about what you will do for a living, you may overlook some opportunities that would be a great fit for your interests and talents. Or you may have a preconceived idea that you have to land one job that pays well and miss the possibility of having two or three vocations going at once.

Spiritually, preconceived ideas may hinder your ability to recognize divine messages and signs. Just as the man in the story of "two boats and a helicopter" didn't recognize that the people offering help from a rowboat, a motorboat, and a helicopter were "angels" sent to help him. When you need help, be aware that the way that your prayer is answered may be very different from what you expected.

Expand your thinking to be open to possibilities. God has much bigger ideas for your life than you can imagine. Do you remember the 1995 song, "One of us" by Joan Osborne with the famous line,

"What if God was one of us"? Many artists, including Alanis Morissette have recorded this song because the lyrics were so powerful. Look up the lyrics and you will remember the theme that God could look like anyone, including a fellow passenger on a bus. Another way of looking at it is that we are all children of God.

When you expand your mind, you realize how much God loves you. Sometimes, when I admire a beautiful sunset with its vivid hues of orange, red, and yellow, I say out loud, "Thank you, God." God is truly a creative artist whose expression of love takes many forms. You can be reminded of God's presence everywhere when you are awestruck at the sight of a beautiful golden harvest moon. God shows love for us in so many ways. Don't miss or take for granted all of the beautiful signs of God's love. Recognize that every beautiful ocean beach and every majestic mountain is a sign of God's power and love.

> *I couldn't find the author of another story about the many ways that God shows his love for you:*
>
> *A man whispered, "God, speak to me." A meadowlark sang, but the man did not hear.*
>
> *Then the man yelled, "God, I can't hear you" and thunder rolled but the man did not listen.*

The man pleaded, "God, let me see you" and a star shone brightly but he did not notice.

Then the man shouted, "God, show me a miracle" and a baby was born, but the man was unaware.

The man cried out in despair, "God, touch me and let me know you are here" and a butterfly landed on his shoulder, but the man brushed it away.

Don't miss blessings because they are not packaged the way that you expect.

Here are some questions to ponder:

1. What ideas do I have that are limiting rather than expanding?
2. What am I missing by having certain expectations for how my life will look?
3. Do I see the spiritual nature of human actions and the beauty of God's work?
4. Has God sent me signs that I missed because they were not what I expected?

You may also have preconceived ideas about success and failure. You may think that your happiness hinges on your attainment of your expected ideas of success. Take some time to define "success" for your life. What are the criteria that you have determined to be important in order for you to be successful?

Let me take this to another level. Have you ever entertained the idea that maybe it would be better to eliminate the concept of "success" altogether? Maybe it would be more constructive to think of achievements in terms of happiness and enjoyment and meaning. Let me give you an example. What if a young man has been working at a major grocery store for years and has no desire to move up the ladder or to change jobs so that he can make more money? What if he tells you sincerely that he is happy working in his position at that store because he loves helping the customers and he likes the other employees. He considers them his "family." If he is still working stocking shelves and bagging groceries when he is 50 years old, would you be tempted to describe him as not being "successful"? Would you think of him as "happy"?

Many of us have preconceived ideas about who is successful and who is not successful. Success unfortunately is often defined as how much money you make, what kind of work you do, and what kind of neighborhood you live in. What if somebody can be perfectly happy with just enough money to keep a very humble roof over their head in a job that does not have high status in our society?

Who decides who is "successful"? These constructs require that someone makes a judgment based on their preconceived ideas. You might complete the phrase, "I'll be happy when I have…"

with some external socially accepted idea like "more money," or "a bigger house" or "a girl-friend." First of all, remember that **your happiness is a choice that you make, regardless of your outside circumstances. You have limited yourself when you only accept socially acceptable ways to be happy.**

Ask yourself what have you learned from society about how to be happy. How about the television commercial with the limiting message that you will enjoy life when you have a certain credit card that can buy you an expensive vacation? Or what about the societal pressure to "fit in"? The very limiting message is that you are happier when you fit in with the crowd. That requires that you change who you really are in order to be socially acceptable.

When I was working on my doctorate at the University of Georgia, one of my class assignments was to spend a day at a "Performance Learning Center" in order to learn about creative ways to be educated. This high school consisted of a principal, a counselor, a secretary, and about 100 students. The students were there because they were not able to learn in a traditional high school.

Many of the students were gifted and, frankly, bored with the structure of everyone learning the same information at the same rate. And I noted during my visit that some were different from the usual students with their green hair and nose rings. Fighting to fit in was not important to them, but being bullied was distracting them from learning. Rather than insisting that these students experience school like everyone else, they were offered an opportunity to learn at their own pace in an accepting environment. By the way, Bill and Melinda Gates contribute money to these Performance Learning Centers all over the nation.

This example has the potential to make many points about limiting, preconceived ideas. Educational concepts can be expanded to include different educational approaches. Ideas about acceptable manners of dress can limit students because they are not allowed to be their authentic selves. **As it pertains to you, limiting your ideas of how to solve problems or how to enjoy yourself or who to bring into your life may also limit your enjoyment of life and your potential happiness. Rather than looking at life in limited ways, make the choice to expand your mind.**

Chapter 23

Reflection

Reflection is an essential strategy in thinking your way to happiness. Take time each day to slow down and reflect on how your day went. **What did you enjoy and what added meaning to your life?** Stop long enough to consider what you want to continue doing and what you want to eliminate.

You can etch out time for reflection in the morning, the afternoon, or the evening. I tend to be a "morning person," so I like to reflect early in the morning with a cup of coffee. During warm weather, I like to sit outside. Many of you may prefer to schedule reflection time at the end of the day, so that the day's events are fresh in your mind. Or you might take a walk after lunch and ponder how the first half of the day went, so that you can make some adjustments for the afternoon and evening.

My point here is "whatever works for you." Just be sure to make time for reflection a part of your daily schedule. It is tempting to get so busy doing, doing, doing and forget that you are not really allowing for time to make changes in your thinking and in your actions. **Make reflection a daily habit.**

THE IMPORTANCE OF REFLECTION

There are many reasons why it is important to take time to reflect. You think happier thoughts when you take the time to remember what you did that gave you a sense of accomplishment. Celebrate every little accomplishment as well as the major achievements. Taking the time to reflect allows you to realize how much you've done well and ways in which you made a difference.

Reflect on your day. What ended up getting the results that you wanted and what didn't work so well? **Think of mistakes as opportunities for learning.** What did you learn from a certain experience? We are all "in process" and we all have the capacity to learn from every experience. Avoid dwelling on errors in judgment. Instead, look at what happened and think of yourself as a student in the school of life.

Another way that reflection is beneficial is that you take the time to generate great ideas. **Reflect on what you want in your life, what you've done, what you are doing, and what you want to do.** If you just keep forging ahead with your life, you might miss opportunities to think of new ways to get what you want.

When I was studying "creativity" as part of my doctoral requirements, I learned that ideas need time to "gel." You might be thinking about ways to change an important aspect of your life. Before you can put the finishing touches on your ideas, it is helpful to give your thoughts time to "gel," and not just rush into action.

Taking the time to let your mind mull over the possibilities and let the creative process play out will be worth the effort. I use this strategy with my gardening and my writing. I may sit on my garden bench and consider various designs for what to plant where. I even make a drawing in pencil. Then I mull it over for a few days before I make a final decision on where to plant the tomatoes, the green beans, and the peppers, for example. When I take time to reflect, then I remember that corn and beans like to live close to each other, but tomatoes don't like to be close to peppers. Then I plant accordingly. Also, when I give my ideas time to "gel," then new ideas come to me.

The same process applies to writing this book. I write a chapter, but it is often not completed until the next day. In the interim, I have reflected on additional content that I want to incorporate or I have decided that one of the paragraphs really isn't relevant and needs to be deleted. So, taking the time to reflect results in a finished product that fits my intentions.

In addition to celebrating your accomplishments, examining possible room for change, and generating ideas, reflection also helps you to take

the time to think of others. You might reflect on what's going on with your family or friends. You might remember that your elderly neighbor mentioned that she's running out of salt. When you slow down, it might occur to you that there are ways that you could be of help to others or that others could be of help to you.

REFLECTION OPENS A SPACE SO THAT YOU CAN PUT EVERYDAY CONCERNS IN PERSPECTIVE.

For example, a high-pressure project at work can seem overwhelming until you take the time to break it down into manageable pieces. When you get overwhelmed, take a few minutes to step back and look at the situation in the bigger scheme of things and then the hurdles don't seem so insurmountable. Reflection can help to calm you down as you gain perspective.

Reflection is a process of examining ourselves, including our thoughts and actions. You can also look more deeply at your **attributes** and what you have to offer that can make a difference. You are a unique person with your own individual gifts and talents. In what ways can your talents be utilized to make a difference in your life and in the lives of others?

When you take the time to reflect, you are giving yourself permission to take a deep breath.

When you do, insights may come into your consciousness that would have been missed. You might gain an understanding of how your life has been unfolding and why. Then you can make changes that add more enjoyment to your life. You can consider whether your daily actions are getting you closer to your life's purpose.

Reflective thinking can also include consideration of the bigger picture. You might be taking the time to explore the meaning of an experience. Maybe you had one of those days when synchronicity merged into your awareness. Now you can reflect on whether you believe the synchronicity of crossing paths with so many kindred spirits that day was a coincidence. Or was there a deeper meaning to connecting with those people?

As you reflect, I suggest that you record some of your thoughts in your journal. Remember that a journal is not the same as a diary because journaling includes the element of reflection. It's amazing how much you can learn about your thinking when you go back over what you have recorded days or weeks before. As you grow and learn, it will be apparent that you have made progress. You will see that your thinking is evolving as you put your new strategies into motion.

When I have looked back over past journal entries, I have sometimes said to myself, "I cannot believe that something that seemed so important to me just a few weeks ago seems so trivial to me now. I have really come a long way toward creating a happier life."

Malcomb Forbes said, *"When what we are is what we want to be, that's happiness."*

Lao Tzu said something similar, *"He who knows others is clever. He who knows himself is enlightened."*

As you make time for reflecting, you are really exploring who you are, what your life looks like, and how you plan to change what does not fit who you are. You are making opportunities to decipher what you like and sort out and rearrange what you don't like. The larger context of your life becomes a more important consideration as you choose what to think about, how to think about it, what to continue doing, and what to change.

On a higher level, you are transforming your life. Transformation is such a challenging and elevating attainment. Years ago, when I got a tattoo on my shoulder, I knew that whatever was permanently inked into my skin had to be meaningful to me. I asked the artist to create a butterfly because of my belief that the transformation of a caterpillar into a butterfly represents one of the most magical examples of transformation, literally and spiritually.

As you reflect in your journal, you are recording your own transformation. And, by writing it down, you are giving yourself tangible credit for what you are working toward. You are recording what you have accomplished as a springboard to what you are looking forward to in the future. This thought brought to mind the importance of having something to look forward to. I remember when I was in junior high, I looked forward to the school dance for weeks. I anticipated how much fun I was going to have and I prepared for the big event by buying a special dress.

It really is crucial to have something to look forward to, isn't it? Your reflections may make it clear to you that you have been so "dug in" to your routine of work or school and taking care of the daily necessities of living that you haven't balanced work with play. You may realize that most of your time has been spent in the pursuit of money or an educational diploma, certificate or degree. That has left little time to relax and have fun.

Happiness includes a balance of the concentration required for necessary endeavors and the nonchalance of letting loose and having a good time. The premise of the entertainment industry is to take you to another reality that doesn't require any work on your part. Music, sports, comedy, and good movies are just a few examples of ways that you can escape the rigors of life and let your mind relax.

I just heard Kelly Clarkston's song, "Just Sing,"

from the new 2020 movie, *"Trolls World Tour."* The lyrics are optimistic and the beat is catchy. Before I knew it, I was bouncing up and down and nodding my head to the music. This is the kind of song that I like to listen to when I walk, because it has a great beat and because it is energizing.

Here are some questions to ponder:

1. What has the process of reflection taught you about yourself?
2. What has surprised you as you compared the content of your past and present journaling?
3. What are you looking forward to in your life?
4. What do you do to balance work and play?

Chapter 24

False Expectations

You will be happier if you don't have false expectations about people, experiences, and life, in general.

False expectations can lead to disappointment and frustration

Have you ever had any of these false expectations? Most of us have had at least some of these illusions:

1. **One false expectation is that life will be easy.** If you've lived long enough, you already know that life is not easy. Life can be hard. If you expect an easy path, you are setting yourself up for lots of frustration. You may find yourself asking, "Why does my life have to be so hard?" What I am going to say in the next sentence may sound ridiculous at first, but give it some time to sink in. **When you accept the fact that life is hard, then it gets easier.** In 1969, the song *"I never promised you a rose garden"* was introduced on a debut album by singer/songwriter, Joe South. The message

of the lyrics was to enjoy the good times in a relationship, because bad times are inevitable. This holds true of life in general, too. Life consists of joy and sorrow. Soak up the times of joy to get you through times of sorrow. You are building a firm foundation to keep you steady.

2. **Another false expectation is that life should be fair.** This includes that people should treat you fairly or events should go the way that you want them to go. You have probably heard people complain that a situation in their life "isn't fair." Maybe you have thought that yourself. The concept of a situation not "being fair" usually refers to one person having an advantage over another. The playing field is not equal. The same rules don't apply to everyone. It is true that everyone does not have the same advantages. The key to staying happy when you are not treated fairly is to look at the situation as objectively as possible and figure out how to get what you want anyway. Complaining about the unfair advantage that someone else has won't get you what you want. Instead, it's better to be clever and figure out how to maneuver through the obstacles and attain your goal.

3. **A third false expectation is that if you are nice to someone, they will be nice to you.**

This is an old cliche' that is not even close to true. Sometimes, you are kind to someone and they return your kindness with indifference or downright meanness. It takes some cunning to discern who will appreciate your kindness and who will not. It is okay if you are not kind to everyone. Actually, this has been a hard life lesson for me. I'll bet it has for you, too. Especially for women, there is the societal expectation that our role is to make everyone comfortable. You know, make sure they have a glass of tea, even if there's none left for you. That sacrificial idea of the martyr still rears it ugly head at times. I hope that we all are kind when we want to be kind, not because it is expected.

4. **Another false expectation is that you should trust everyone.** It is better to let people earn your trust than to just blindly trust anyone. **Have you noticed that, in general, some people give more than they take and other people take more than they give?** I don't mean once in a while. I mean that there is a definite pattern. Also, takers tend to seek out givers. It's like we have a sign on our foreheads that says, "It's okay to take from me. I give generously." So, be careful. If you know that you tend to be giving, be on guard for someone who wants to take from you. Sometimes, those

of us who tend to give more than we take are not discerning about when it is beneficial to give of our time, energy, and money. I have certainly fallen into this trap more than once in my life. It is a tough lesson to learn when you want to think the best of everyone. We have been raised to give everyone the benefit of the doubt. I have learned, though, that it can save you a lot of heartache when you say, "No." It may save you some of your hard-earned money, too.

If you looked at your life like a movie with you as the main character, how would you see yourself? Would you be a person who adheres to false expectations, and then suffers from frustration, disappointment, and even rage? Or would you spend your time navigating your life with a keen awareness that some people will be insincere and don't deserve your kindness or your trust? When you see life realistically, you are not as shocked, surprised, or knocked off course every time life presents unfair situations or scheming people.

One of the main themes of this book is that you cannot rely on external events and people for your happiness. Let's take that a step further. Developing a shrewd awareness of what's going on outside of your life and acting accordingly will save you a lot of wasted time and, hopefully, you won't be saying, "I can't believe that just happened to me."

We set ourselves up for false expectations and then we judge ourselves based on something that we are not even capable of...

> *For example, we mistakenly believe:*
> *I can stop someone from abusing drugs or alcohol.*
> *I can make someone trust herself.*
> *I can make someone angry.*
> *I can hurt someone's feelings.*
> *I can control events around me.*
> *I can make someone happy.*

Remember, you cannot control other people's emotions or their actions. Parents cannot control their children and they cannot make them happy. The consequence of not realizing this bit of wisdom is that many parents blame themselves when their children take actions that have negative consequences.

The same applies to anyone. Remember, you cannot control anyone but yourself and you cannot make someone happy. Their happiness or unhappiness is their choice. Because we live under these illusions, we tend to feel guilty when anyone, including our own children, are having a hard time. Hopefully, when we realize that we have a lot of false expectations for ourselves and others, we can begin to take responsibility only for our own life.

Here's a quote from *The Four Agreements Companion Book*, a sequel to the very popular book by don Miguel Ruiz:

> *"Nothing others do is because of you. What others say and do is a projection of their own reality, their own dream. When you are immune to the opinions and actions of others, you won't be the victim of needless suffering."*

The reality is that people are doing what they choose to do and life events are unfolding, whether you like it or not. Some people who are "lost souls" are really seeking guidance and will benefit from your help and some people who seem to be "lost souls" in need of your help will ignore your advice and continue on their merry way.

How you choose to respond to external events is determined, in part, by your perception of reality. When your beliefs correlate with reality, you are going to have a much smoother journey through life.

There are people who just coast through life, taking from others and giving little, if anything, in return. Lucky for them that there are so many people willing to enable them to avoid responsibility. Remember, everything that you do is your choice. And it follows that everything that other people do is their choice.

Others may blame you for their misfortunes or transgressions. It is better for your peace of mind if you choose to ignore their accusations. A lot of people will deny their part in their own difficulties and look for a scapegoat. Here's where it is best to just walk away or hang up the phone and not listen to their false accusations.

Another illusion that we sometimes live by pertains to our relationship with God. We might live with the illusion that when things don't happen the way we want, we think that God has forsaken us. This is not true. God is constantly in our lives. What we forget is that God has bigger ideas for our lives than we can imagine. What we think is best may not be what God knows to be best.

As you think about how false expectations affect your life, you might ask yourself these questions:

1. What am I really responsible for?
2. What can I control in my life?
3. What explanation do I give when things don't go the way I want?
4. What false expectations do I have?

Chapter 25

Feeling Overwhelmed

When I was leading discussions in the Ellijay, Georgia, personal growth groups, I would often begin our time together with an opening statement that would set the mood. The gatherings were in the evenings and I realized that many of the women were coming directly from a hard day at work.

I wanted to help them leave the day's busyness behind and focus only on taking care of themselves. If space permitted, I had a candle on a table in the middle of the circle. And I had created an agenda for the evening that included a theme, a quote, discussion points, and some questions to encourage sharing in the "talking circle."

The theme for one evening was "Feeling Overwhelmed" and the main points in this chapter come from that evening's agenda.

Here is an opening statement that I read to help the women feel comfortable:

> "We are here together to nourish one another. We do that by listening to each other, offering support and encouragement.

The candle on the table symbolizes Light. Light and joy.

It is here, among friends, that you can relax and be yourself. You are taking some time just for you. You can be your authentic self here…no need to please or to hold back feelings.

You don't have to DO anything here. We will be together for a while. We will be with ourselves and with each other. This is time for you…to be yourself, to be true to yourself."

My quote for the Feeling Overwhelmed theme was from *A Course in Miracles,* a 1976 book that became wildly popular. I had previously participated in a series of meetings in *A Course in Miracles* and was inspired by the premise of being aware of love's presence in our lives. This particular quote seemed to fit with our theme.

"Every situation, properly perceived, becomes an opportunity to heal." (A Course in Miracles, Helen Schucman, 1976).

I know that every one of you has felt totally overwhelmed, probably many times in your life. Maybe you feel overwhelmed right now. I can't tell you how many times I have been so overwhelmed that I went right into the "fight or flight" response, which for me would be "flight." I would avoid or attempt to escape from whatever felt like almost more stress than I could handle.

From a woman's perspective, feeling overwhelmed is a by-product of a multitude of responsibilities

Responsibilities that contribute to feeling overwhelmed include work, family, housework, buying groceries, cooking, and on and on it goes. Then add money worries, and it could bring you almost to a breaking point. And don't forget relationship issues, which torment us because we feel that it is our place to fix them.

I have heard many women say, "I just want to run away sometimes." I'll bet many of you have said the same thing. I know I have. It all just feels like too much. But here you are, feeling trapped by a situation and wondering how to change it.

Years ago, I ran across a movie called "Land of Little Rain," starring Helen Hunt. It was inspired by the true story of Mary Austin (1868-1934), who was a writer. Mary wrote fondly about the beauty of the southwestern United States and of the Native American people who lived there. Before her writing career became prominent in her life, she was married to a man who was a bit of a dreamer. He was an interesting man, following many pursuits, but never able to settle on anything long enough to support his wife and daughter.

Mary was desperate to make money, after they

were evicted from their apartment and all their belongings were put in the street. In 1900, even with her college degree, she could not get a teaching job without permission from her husband. And he was gone most of the time.

She finally got a teaching job, but that meant that she had to have her daughter with her when she couldn't get help. Her daughter had behavioral and emotional difficulties, often going into tantrums and screaming until she was exhausted. At least that's the way she was portrayed in the movie. Also, Mary's love of the Indian culture was looked down on by the more prominent members of the community, making it even harder to find employment.

Mary was obviously feeling overwhelmed. Finally, she became so distraught that she broke down and yelled to a friend, "I'm holding onto some dream of a family. It's the aloneness of it. That's what's so frightening. That's the reality." After she blurted out her distress, she came to terms with the necessity of letting go. She let go of her husband by getting a divorce. She eventually let go of her daughter by taking her to a home for disturbed children.

Eventually, Mary found an artist's group where she fit in and flourished. Her writings began to be published in magazines after she found a niche where she was welcomed and appreciated.

The story of Mary Austin may seem to be an extreme example of feeling overwhelmed, but **I bet that many of you can relate to the feelings of being overwhelmed that she experienced.** You are struggling to juggle all the pieces of your life, and you can't figure out how to find some peace of mind.

LETTING GO
REQUIRES A PARADIGM SHIFT

By "letting go," I don't necessarily mean literally letting go, like Mary Austin did. I am referring to letting go and allowing ourselves to be inspired and guided by God. Taking time to hit the "pause" button is more difficult than just saying, "Let go and let God." We are so used to attempting to control events and other people that it can feel strange and maybe a bit frightening to be still and listen for guidance.

This requires a paradigm shift, a big change in our thinking about how life works. Trusting that we are a vital part of a universal web of existence and that answers will come when we just open ourselves up and listen is not how we were taught to operate in our society. We are supposed to figure it out and take charge. Or, just suck it up. You know the saying, "You made your bed, now lay in it."

Yet, the best ideas come in quiet solitude. So,

how are you going to schedule "alone time" for yourself? First, put yourself on the calendar. You might call it "Me time."

When you feel overwhelmed, you know that you must let go of something, whether it's a way of thinking or something tangible. But what?

Sometimes we are overwhelmed because we have taken on too much. So, the question is, "What are you going to stop doing?" It can be hard to say, "No!" But you know that you cannot continue to operate at such a maddening pace.

Another strategy when you feel overwhelmed is to figure out how you can spend your time more efficiently. Can you schedule your time so that you take care of similar tasks in one block of time? An obvious example is answering emails. Just pick a time and look at them only once a day.

Errands are another example. Plan all of your stops in advance so that you make sort of a circle, to go everywhere that it is necessary to go. This is after you have thought about what can be done online or by mail. I still pay a lot of bills by check because it forces me to record the transaction in my paper register, so later I don't say, "Now where did I spend that money?"

I recently discovered that I can buy stamps at Walmart at the same time that I buy groceries. Or I can buy them online. In other words, I don't have to make a separate trip to the Post Office. As I focus on my goal of completing this book and getting my garden planted, I am more aware of all the distractions that get me off track.

So, I am letting go of the inefficiencies that add to my stress and take away from achieving my goals. The best master of getting things done in the least amount of time is Timothy Ferriss. His book, *"The 4-Hour Workweek"* is a reference book for me. Not only have I read it, but I keep referring back to it for inspiration and "nuts and bolts" ideas on time management. I highly recommend this book.

Another issue that can lead to feeling overwhelmed is interruptions. The best strategy is to schedule your day and stick to it. Since I am at home working, it is tempting for people to think that I am available any ole time. I still am not 100 % great at avoiding interruptions, but I'm doing better. And, guess what, I'm getting a lot more done in a lot less time.

Strategies like scheduling your day, avoiding interruptions, and eliminating what is not absolutely necessary get you back to feeling more in control of your life. You are putting yourself first, spending time on your priorities, and letting go of what you can. I guess the opposite of feeling overwhelmed is feeling calm and having peace of mind. Here's to feeling less distracted and living a more tranquil life.

Chapter 26

Your Spiritual Self

Your soul craves a deep, rich, meaningful experience of life. Take the time to slow down and think about your spiritual life. When you shift your thinking to making your spirituality more of a priority, then you will create a relationship with God. You will experience more of a sense of awe at the wonders of life. You will feel more grateful, more accepting, and more peaceful. The possibilities offered by the present moment will be more apparent.

You are going toward having more faith, more hope, and more courage. You will be more inquisitive about the daily miracles in your life and more enthusiastic about your spiritual growth. The "unexplained" now takes up a lot of your thinking as you relish in the synchronicities that validate your interconnectedness with all of existence.

YOUR JOURNEY INWARD
MAY BE FULL OF SURPRISES

You are about to experience a cheerful journey into the inner you. Delightful surprises await you as you open yourself to a heightened awareness of the spiritual. One of the fun parts of being connected with the women in the personal growth groups was that they would constantly surprise me with the depth of their spirituality…and their cleverness.

When I suggested giving the Dawsonville group a name, the women took that suggestion and ran with it. The Dawsonville women called their group the "Meadowlarks: A cheerful journey inward." Those inquisitive ladies researched the symbolism of the bird, the meadowlark, in Ted Andrews' book, *Animal Speak: The Spiritual and Magical Powers of Creatures Great and Small.* They enthusiastically shared with the group that, according to the author, many of the meadowlark's behaviors reflect the inward journey and movement often associated with self-discovery. The author referred to the lark as a symbol of the ability to divert energy from an immediate goal to one of a higher social and moral level. The meadowlark, he wrote, can teach us that the process of going inward can be filled with joy. Hence, the logo, "Cheerful Journey Inward."

The Ellijay women chose to call their group the "Butterflies: transforming our lives through personal growth." I was so blessed to spend many inspiring evenings with these women. They were eager to learn and to grow and initiated pushing themselves to expand their lives. Some initiated learning about metaphysical subjects like auras and one woman even took classes in remote viewing.

One evening we met at one of the women's homes so that we could watch a video based on a local author's book about changes in the environment. Another time, Doris Helge, the author of the book, *Transforming Pain into Power*, accepted my invitation to speak to our group. What a life-changing night that was. Thank you, Doris!

You can have fun with your adventures into self-discovery. Delving into the spiritual realm will lift your spirit to heights that you could not imagine before you became aware of spiritual experiences.

Maybe you can work toward finding spiritual significance in more facets of your life. When you pay more attention to your spiritual life, you see more evidence of the divine in everyday events. Let me give you an example from my life.

Years ago, I received a letter from a friend in which he referenced the life of a dragonfly. He shared that the dragonfly lives most of its life in larval form under the water before rising into the air to share its beauty for a short time. This year, I passed on these inspiring words to some family members in an email.

One week later, I walked out on the porch and a huge dragonfly was on a round orange table by the door. Larry had found it stuck to a wall in a new construction site where he was working. Even though it had died, he brought it to me because he

Laurie Hyatt, Ph.D.

knows that I see the sacred in dragonflies. That synchronicity was a spiritual experience for me. I know that divine intervention was involved in the "coincidence" of writing about a dragonfly and then one appearing in my life.

Don't miss opportunities for delight as you search for the sacred in your life. Experiences like this remind you that you are connected to all living things.

This spiritual sign reminded me of a bit of wisdom from author, Alan Cohen, in his book, *"The Dragon Doesn't Live Here Anymore: Living Fully, Loving Freely."* The author wrote:

> *"When you take one step toward God, He takes ten steps toward you."*

THINK OF EVERYTHING IN LIFE AS A VAST SYSTEM OF ENERGY.

All of life is a vast system of energy. You will receive an inpouring of spiritual energy when you change your perception of life. Focus your thoughts on the bigger picture, especially when you are tempted to get drawn into conflict or dramas. Turn your attention to the spiritual and see yourself as getting energy from a Higher Source.

Remember that you are a spiritual being in a human body. An excellent illustration of this concept was given by Neale Donald Walsch, author of the *Conversations with God* trilogy, during a presentation in Marietta, Georgia. After enthusiastically devouring his books, I was excited about the opportunity to learn from the author. I learned that he was a fascinating and thought-provoking speaker. My daughter, Heather, and I laughed a lot and were mesmerized by the combination of his teachings with accompanying music.

The presenter's point was that Who We Really Are is not the superficial aspects of our lives or the roles that we play. He made the point brilliantly with funny stories from his own life. Even though he received recognition for his hair, his car, and his pretty girlfriend, they did not define his true identify. He also was not his family or his job, which he discovered when they were gone. When he was stripped of his possessions, his relationships, and his job, he realized that his true self remained. This kind of self-discovery can lead you to look deeper at your spiritual self.

When you begin to **live your life from the inside out**, it shakes things up a bit. What was important is no longer important. What defined you before this shift in perspective is no longer what defines you. And how you see the world changes radically.

When my daddy died in 1981, I was shaken to the core, even though he had been ill for years. I journaled a lot through the first weeks of grief. The perspective that we are all spiritual beings in human bodies became clear. I had an interesting experience when I was at the airport, before boarding a plane to take daddy's ashes to be buried in Connecticut. As I looked out at all of the people going their separate ways to their individual destinations, I didn't think about where they were all going, which used to fascinate me. After this tragic loss, I shifted my perspective and focused my attention on the souls, rather than the bodies.

Our spirits run our lives from the inside out. Our spirits search for opportunities to grow and serve and create platforms for change. Our spiritual self sees existence as a gift from God and is grateful. Our "spiritual self" searches out ways to live according to our highest idea of ourselves.

The three levels of communication between humans are heart to heart, mind to mind, and soul to soul. True intimacy is revealed in soulful conversation. **To develop a soulful dialogue with God, we must listen more than we talk.**

GOD'S MESSAGES ARE REVEALED IN UNEXPECTED WAYS.

God wants to give you clarity. God can give you strength. When we spend quiet, uninterrupted time every day expressing our gratitude, God smiles. When we ask for direction, God guides us.

The relationship between our spiritual self and God is a two-way street. We talk, God listens. God talks, we listen. Don't tell God what you want or need. Ask God, "What do you want me to do?" When you ask in all sincerity, you may be amazed at how quickly God responds.

When you are self-absorbed with your daily activities, you miss out on all the messages that God is sending you. Be open to the many ways that God communicates with you.

Years ago, my car was damaged when a big truck side-swiped me on a narrow street. The insurance company sent out an adjuster to assess the damage. We exchanged greetings, he looked at the car, and told me where to take my car for repairs. Then, I was shocked when he said that he had a book that he was supposed to give me. Now, keep in mind that we had never met before and we did not have any mutual friends. This was a complete stranger.

He quickly explained that he received a "message" to give me the book, *STARSEED: The Third Millenium: Living in the Posthistoric World* by Ken Carey. When he returned the next day, he gave me the necessary paperwork for the repair shop, and then he handed me a copy of the book. It was all very surreal. I soon learned as I read the book that it was what I would call a cosmic spiritual guide.

As I reflected on that spiritual experience, I was

reminded of something that Jerry Ellis shared in his book, *Walking the Trail: One Man's Journey Along the Cherokee Trail of Tears.* Let me give you some background. The author walked the 900-mile Trail of Tears and had many spiritual experiences along the way. One day, he was walking across a street in a small town, when a man approached him and shared a profound message. Just out of the blue. Frankly, I can't remember the content right now, but it was one of those serendipitous moments.

I have now made a note to myself to buy another copy of the book and read it again. Yes, it's that good. According to Jerry Ellis, the walk was full of meaningful experiences. He noted that most people were really kind to him and that he was only afraid once, and that was because of a misconception on his part.

My wish for you is that you experience the delight and wonder of being a part of a much greater reality that is full of surprises. It's like a mystery that you can't quite figure out, but you know that your spiritual self is playing a really important part.

Chapter 27

Breaking Out of the Box

You break out of the box of limitations when you radically shift your thinking from "This is what my life is" to "This is what my life could be." Before shifting your thinking, you have been trapped in a dark, confining box labeled "This is all there is." You have not been happy living within the walls of the box, but you saw no way out.

Then an inkling of sunlight streams through a fold in the box top. You are fascinated with the bright light. It suddenly occurs to you that there are possibilities for happiness outside the box. You decide to free yourself by pushing toward the light.

Positive thoughts flood your mind. Opportunities to be your authentic self and live the life that you choose for yourself are revealed. You feel energy surge through your body, mind, and spirit. You are giving yourself permission to live the life of your dreams.

My very personal reason for believing that it is important to break out of the box and experience freedom is my Daddy. I began the Acknowledgments section of my 2001 book, *Tools for Living*, by saying:

"Special thanks to...

Daddy, who had the idea to break out of the box."

After Daddy died when I was 34 years old, I found a letter that he had written to a friend when I was a senior in college. He explained that he planned to head to Port Aransas, Texas, to be a beachcomber after I finished my bachelor's degree. But he was postponing his plans because I had decided to go on for my Master's degree. I didn't know about his dream of beachcombing, but I wish I had. I would have said, "Daddy, you and Mother go on to the beach. I'll figure out how to pay for graduate school."

Daddy had spent years working to support his family. He had hung in there when the company he worked for was bought out in a corrupt way and people were fired or demoted from the top down. He did not enjoy his job after that. In fact, he was angry that the company's president, who Daddy considered to be a good friend, was fired. Daddy no longer had the opportunities to write newsletter feature columns and build relationships with the community as the head of Public Relations. He was transferred to Technical Writer, a position that did not acknowledge his creativity.

That would have been a good time for Daddy to break out of the box. But concerns about financial obligations won out. I certainly understand that, but I watched as he lost his soul to that company. He lost his zest for living. I have wished a thousand times that he had just told his employer to "shove it" and walked out. A simple life in the sun and sand would probably have kept his passion for life ignited. He would have enjoyed walking the beach, fishing, and living with Nature. He loved to fish and sunbathe. Finding treasures from the sea would have given his life meaning. He would have thought happy thoughts as he filled his bucket or baited his hook.

Probably like many of you, I have worked many jobs that I literally detested just to make the money necessary to survive. I'm certainly not advocating impulsively leaving a job or a relationship or a residence on a whim. **I am suggesting that you take the time to brainstorm possibilities for an enjoyable and meaningful life and figure out how to make it happen.**

Society has a way of zapping "free spirits," adventurers, and seekers. It tries to get us to conform and when we don't, we are branded as "irresponsible" or "selfish." The traditional conformists who adhere to society's rules, stay in the same job, live in the same neighborhood, keep the same relationships are considered to be responsible adults and good citizens. Being intense and passionate and spontaneous is labeled "irresponsible," "reckless," and "immature." Being steady, consistent, and predictable is admired. Changing jobs every few years is judged negatively.

If you are a free spirit, a curious, artistic, creative idea generator, and you attempt to survive in an environment of routine, rules, and dogma, it kills your spirit. Not being valued for Who You Really Are breeds resentment and a feeling that you are invisible. This is a result of years of being discounted, de-valued, and misunderstood.

It begins when you are told as children to stay "inside the lines" when you draw. And that picture of an apple better be colored red. You and I have been told not to use our imaginations. The message is, "Don't consider other possibilities." Yet some of you keep bucking the system and you keep getting slapped down. And, yes, you can lose your will. Your spirit can die.

Being valued is an energy booster. Being treated with respect, as if your ideas are important, adds to your enjoyment of life. Being with like-minded people is energizing. I met a woman the other day who I knew was a "kindred spirit" the minute we started talking. She is a craftswoman who has a very innovative flair for renovating old furniture. I noticed that my energy level increased exponentially while she was showing me her works of art.

FREE SPIRITS HAVE TO FLY.

I hope that you burst out of that limiting box that is filled with "should's" and soar away toward new ideas and dreams. Just like plants, you need energy in order to grow. If plants don't get enough light energy from the sun, they get leggy and spindly and then wither and die. Plants that are exposed to lots of sunlight are sturdy.

You are just like those plants. You thrive when you come out into the light. You **break out of that dark, confining box** of limiting thoughts and open yourself to new ways of thinking and fresh ideas. Your new mantra is "I can't wait to see what today will bring."

Remember the book, *Jonathon Livingston Seagull,* by Richard Bach? The story is about a seagull who flies high for the sheer enjoyment of flying, while his family judges him and actually sends him away. They admonish him because, according to their limiting rules, the sole purpose of flying is to retrieve fish to eat. Jonathon had broken out of the box when he felt the exhilaration of doing all kinds of dives and loops for the sheer pleasure of feeling free. If you've read the book, you know that the flock finally came around and learned from him that you can fly to get food and you can also fly for the sheer pleasure of soaring.

Open your heart, and you reveal your authentic self. Expand your mind, and you ponder big ideas. Lift your spirit, and you communicate with God.

When you break out of the box, you see the

world from the perspective of your spiritual self. **You run your life from the inside out.** Gone are the days of pleasing others and looking to others for validation. **You are in the driver's seat of your life.**

WHEN YOU **OPEN YOUR HEART**, YOU KNOW WHO YOU REALLY ARE. You have taken the time to be honest with yourself about what's really important to you. You have assessed your interests and talents. You have developed goals and prioritized them. You have asked yourself this question:

- **What do I really want to do?**

WHEN YOU EXPAND YOUR MIND, YOUR IMAGINATION TAKES OFF. You are no longer filling your mind with what others are doing. You are in control of what you think about. Now you ask yourself this question:

- **What do I want to learn?**

WHEN YOU LIFT YOUR SPIRIT, you feel lighter and more carefree. You realize the importance of your spiritual life. You see yourself as connected to all living beings. You have a vital purpose in the creative process. You ask yourself:

- **How can I grow spiritually?**

Chapter 28

Freedom

Freedom has been a goal for me for as long as I can remember. When I was 20 years old, I earned my private pilots license. There were two reasons why I wanted to fly airplanes. First, I was fascinated by Daddy's enthusiasm for flying. As a newspaperman in Connecticut, he wrote a series of feature stories on aviation and took some lessons himself to add personal interest. Second, I really wanted to soar up into the wild blue yonder, which seemed to me to be the ultimate freedom.

After I flew with an instructor for about ten sessions, I was free to fly solo. How exhilarating it was to realize that I was up in the sky, just me and a Cessna 150, completely detached from the earth. I looked down to see fields and houses and streams, which looked small from my lofty perspective high above. **I was free to fly.** Let me add that I also realized that the only one who could get me safely back down to earth was me, only me. But the thrill of flying filled my heart and soul and far outweighed the fear.

FREEDOM IS
SELF-DETERMINATION

When you are free, you are not under the control or power of anyone but yourself. More important, you have freed yourself from the self-imposed restrictions that you used to put on yourself. You love yourself. You care about yourself.

You choose to be free to follow what's really important to you. You see the world with a much clearer, broader lens. You have let go of your old views of life and have shifted your thinking to the bigger picture.

Now, you feel optimistic that you can meet any challenge with a solution. Just like the rocks in the river analogy, you can go over or around whatever gets in the way of your progress. As part of the requirements to get my pilots license, I had to complete a number of solo cross-country trips where I flew to a designated location, landed, got a signature from someone to verify that I had landed there, and then fly back to the Arlington, Texas, airport.

Well, wouldn't you know that on my first cross-country trip, I was flying right toward a big rain cloud. I had not flown in rain, so I decided to fly around the clouds. As I navigated around the storm, I checked my compass and watched for check points to find the assigned airport. I have to admit that I breathed a sigh of relief when that airport came in view. I had accomplished my goal, and it was fun sharing my experience with my instructor when I got back.

With your new insight and confidence, you create a sense of calm that allows you to observe whatever is going on without freaking out or jumping to conclusions. You can give yourself time to be with a situation before you make a decision. You can consider all of your options and choose the solution that you think will get you to your goal.

You are free to be your authentic self. **You are free** to pursue your own interests and passions to bring enjoyment to your own life, and perhaps to the lives of others.

Needing validation from others is a behavior that no longer serves you. Now **you** determine that you have self-worth. Pleasing others is a waste of your time. You don't need to prove yourself to anyone or to justify your ideas or behaviors. Not concerning yourself with other people's opinion of you may feel strange at first. But you're getting the hang of it and a huge burden is lifted from your shoulders.

Because you know **Who You Really Are**, you can let go of any relationship, job, or situation that doesn't align with your authentic self. For example, if your company values profit to the point of detriment to the client, and that doesn't align with your values, you can leave. That has happened to me several times. One time, my place of employment was taken over by a firm who came in and told me that from that day forward I would be spending my time on the phone getting insurance payments instead of having individual therapy with the young clients. They were not going to offer the individual therapy sessions anymore, because it was not cost-effective. They would let me continue the group therapy sessions, because they made a ton of money charging the insurance companies for each person in the group. I was looking for a new job the next day.

FREEDOM IS BEING YOURSELF

You know that you are not perfect, and you realize that perfection isn't the goal. Although you still put lots of thought and planning into your efforts because you are conscientious, you realize that you will make mistakes. And that's okay. In fact, if you aren't making some mistakes, you aren't out there really experiencing life.

Vulnerability can be shared, because you know that you are worthy of love. Actually, when you share your authentic self, including your doubts and fears, with others, an opportunity for deeper connection appears. I guess that's one reason why most of us like stories of the "flawed hero" because we can relate to that person.

My favorite character in the *Game of Thrones* books was Tyrion. He spent a lot of time reading and thinking because he had a physical challenge and couldn't joust on horseback like other men. He was very direct with people and he got things done. But he had this weakness for women that would cause him to make the stupidest decisions and take far too many chances. Even though I would chastise him out loud as I read, I liked him because he wasn't portrayed by the author as being perfect. Even though Tyrion was brilliant, he could still act foolishly.

When **you are free** to be yourself, you can follow your passions and do what contributes to your happiness. You can be creative, imaginative, and express your true feelings without worrying about negative comments made by others. Remember that some of the most innovative humans on this planet have been mocked and made fun of for their ideas, until those ideas led to huge breakthroughs that changed human lives for the better.

Live in the moment and feel free to just be. You don't have to be doing, doing, doing all the time. Dan Harris, in collaboration with Jeff Warren and Carlye Adler, encouraged his readers to take the time to meditate in a really funny and informative book titled, *Meditation for Fidgety Skeptics*. He delightfully shared his difficulties with letting go of his thoughts about work, for example, so that he could empty his mind. I hope you read it.

You achieve freedom when you shift your perspective about why an issue or a person has come into your life. For example, instead of being upset about the shelter-in-place mandates accompanying the present concern over the COVID-19 virus, I am grateful that I can take the time to write without interruption. While others are going stir-crazy, I am basking in the opportunity to stay home and work. This has come easy to me.

I have to admit that the issue that I continue to fight rather than shifting my perspective is my high blood pressure. I did have a revelation today that it would be better to look at it as a reminder to eat healthy, walk regularly, and relax often. When I frame it as a source of information rather than something that I have to control, perhaps some of the pressure will be alleviated. I have not freed myself from anxiety about my blood pressure. Like you, I am a work in progress.

I hope that you realize that I am not writing this book because I think I have mastered all of the concepts. Oh, no. I have a long way to go. Actually, writing this book has heightened my awareness. I have taken the time to reflect and contemplate. I have made some changes in my thinking, and I am definitely still learning.

FREEDOM IS
SPIRITUAL AWARENESS

As you eliminate the baggage and clutter in your life, you free yourself to spend time on your spiritual life. You appreciate the sacredness of your life and how fortunate you are to be spending time here with beautiful Mother Earth. Time that you previously spent complaining is now spent sharing your gratitude with God.

You are free to have interactive dialogues with God where you take the time not only to express your gratitude and ask for guidance, but most importantly to listen. You know that you are an integral force in the creation process and you welcome the opportunity to learn what God intends for your life.

You see yourself as a spiritual being in a human body, which frees you up to spend more time focusing on the true Source of your life and energy and less time on the mundane daily activities that often distract you. Since you have figured out what is important to you, you are now aware that your spiritual life comes first.

You are free to devote time every day to your spiritual evolvement. When I lived alone in a little log cabin in Ellijay, Georgia, I really began to work on my spiritual growth. I began with something tangible that I could literally do every day to get me started. I bought the *Sacred Path Cards: The Discovery of Self through Native Teachings,* created by Jamie Sams. Every day I would sit at my white pine rectangular table and spread the cards. Then I would pick one, trusting that I had chosen the lesson that would benefit me that day.

I learned to nurture myself, to listen for the revealing of my purpose, to show gratitude, and to develop individual goals, among many other lessons. Since I have started writing this book, I ordered a new set of the cards to refresh myself on the teachings. I recommend that you free up some time every day to engage in some kind of ritualistic activity that furthers your spiritual growth.

In my personal experience, it is helpful to have something tangible like whatever cards resonate with you or a book that you read each day.

Taking time to communicate with God or to be present in Nature can be difficult if you don't have the structure to help you get going. I suggest that you say to yourself, "Every evening I will choose a card, read it, and take time to apply the lesson to my life." Or you can tell yourself, "Every morning I will read from a book that has a meditation for each day of the year."

Some of you may take a few minutes every day to read a chapter of the Holy Bible or some other holy book. You can add some structure by starting at the beginning and reading a chapter each day.

Or you may choose to close your eyes and open the Bible, and read the passages that appear where the pages fell open.

You can also feel free to take some time to join a Bible class or a spiritual growth group. Or you may find a "Mind, Body, Spirit" type of speaker's conference in your area. Many authors of books about spiritual growth travel the country giving talks and signing books. You could also take the time to participate in a spiritual retreat for a day, a weekend, or longer.

Now that you are on your way toward your spiritual evolvement, verbalize your intention by saying it out loud, writing it down, or adding it to your prayer talk. I believe that when you put your intentions out to the universe, that message is received and it will be answered. Remember from the story about the two boats and a helicopter that your requests may not materialize in exactly the way that you had imagined. That's the powerful mystery of the spiritual realm.

Now that you are on the path toward freedom, you will be amazed at what shows up. Messengers take many forms. People, books, movies, a bird or a tree. I just saw an inspiring episode in the television series, "Tales from the Loop." In this episode, a little boy was forlorn after his grandfather passed away. Before he died, his wise grandfather taught him to always remember that there is light in the darkness. Looking for some validation of his grandfather's wisdom, the little boy went to a place where they had been together. There he saw dozens of fireflies glowing in the darkness. There was the light in the darkness, as his grandfather said.

You are free to bring light into your life. You can enjoy satisfying relationships and fulfilling work. You can decide what you will do, where you will go, and even know why you are making those choices. You are free to decide what thoughts you will entertain and what thoughts you will eliminate. You are free to decide who you will spend your time with and who you will choose to let go.

You are free to be with people who lift you up and to avoid those who bring you down. You can choose people, activities, and places that add to your enjoyment of life. You can dig deep and discover meaningful experiences that add depth to your life.

YOU ARE FREE TO CHOOSE HAPPINESS!

RECOMMENDED READING

I have decided to recommend just three books to help you add to your happiness. In the beginning of the book, I introduced you to my mantra…

Open Your Heart. Expand Your Mind. Lift Your Spirit.

I have selected books that will help you to celebrate your authentic self, develop goals from great big dreams, and learn how to just BE so that your spirit can take flight. I hope that you enjoy reading them, find them to be a meaningful use of your time, and experience a happier life as a result.

The life-changing magic of tidying up: the Japanese art of decluttering and organizing written with sensitivity and compassion by Marie Kondo. The author doesn't just teach what to discard and what to keep in your home by asking the question, "Does this bring me joy?" As testimonials make clear, many of her followers have changed their thinking and their whole outlook on life.

The 4-Hour Workweek: Escape 9-5, Live Anywhere, and join the New Rich which

Laurie Hyatt, Ph.D.

Timothy Ferriss wrote in a very energetic, very "nuts and bolts" style full of very specific ideas. I keep this book as a reference book, and I continue to read it and read it again. The author pushes the audience to set goals based on expansive ideas and almost unimaginable dreams. He truly inspires as he teaches.

Meditation for Fidgety Skeptics: A 10% Happier How-to Book, written by Dan Harris with the help of Jeff Warren and Carlyle Adler, is a really funny, uplifting, and honest approach to the art of meditation. His teaching is interspersed with actual meditations and fascinating personal stories. "Slow down, relax, and be happy" rings clear in an earnest sharing of missteps and successes. This book is informative and entertaining.

HEALTH TRACKER

Date: _____

NUTRITION

Breakfast	Lunch	Dinner	Snacks

Water: 1 2 3 4 5 6 7 8

Veggies:	Fruits:	Dairy:
1 2 3	1 2	1 2 3
Grains:	**Protein:**	**Fats:**
1 2	1 2	1 2

EXERCISE

Walking (steps and miles):

_____

Weights (pounds and repetitions):

_____

Laurie Hyatt, Ph.D.

Relaxation, "Me Time" (one hour daily)

Goals for this week (steps, miles, foods)

_____

_____

_____

_____

_____

_____

_____

_____

_____

_____

_____

_____

_____

_____

_____

_____

_____

_____

ACKNOWLEDGMENTS

Many people have contributed to the completion of this book and I am grateful to you all.

All of the women who participated in the personal growth groups in Ellijay, Dawsonville, and Gainesville, Georgia, contributed by motivating me and pushing me to think deeper. They shared their experiences and their challenges, and, together, we brainstormed ideas.

Friends and family have read chapters as I wrote, proofreading and making helpful suggestions. My walking buddy, Barbara Wilson, proofread chapters and made encouraging comments. My daughters, Heather and Laurie Grace, read chapters and made suggestions along the way. In addition, Heather, put her analytical skills to work coordinating a marketing plan. Laurie Grace focused her artistic talents on creating the cover design. Larry listened with interest as I read chapters out loud to him to see how the words flowed.

The staff at Booklogix have been professional and efficient in getting the book from a manuscript to a paperback and Kindle books. What a great team!

Many others probably don't realize how helpful they have been by showing interest in what I was

Laurie Hyatt, Ph.D.

writing and saying they couldn't wait to read the finished product.

To everyone who has contributed to my thoughts and who has reinforced the importance of my ideas, thank you.